Oh Brother!

This script is published by
DCG Publications.

All inquiries regarding purchase of further scripts and current royalty rates should be addressed to:

DCG Media Group
Vamos 73008
Chania
Crete
Greece

Email: info@dcgmediagroup.com
www.dcgmediagroup.com

Conditions

- ❖ All DCG Publication scripts are fully protected by the copyright acts. Under no circumstances must they be reproduced by photo-copying or any other means, either in whole or in part.

- ❖ The license to perform referred to above only relates to live performances of this script. A separate license is required for video-taping or sound recording, which will be issued on receipt of the appropriate fee.

- ❖ The name of the author shall be clearly stated on all publicity, programs etc. The program credits shall state "Script provided by DCG Publications".

Oh Brother!

By

Glyn Jones

DCG
Publications

First Published in Greece 2010

© Glyn Jones

The author's moral rights have been asserted

DCG Publications
www.dcgmediagroup.com

ISBN 978-960-99470-2-2

Typeset by
DCG Publications

Printed in England by
Lightning Source.

First Produced
at the

Ipswich Theatre
Ipswich

July 10th 1962

Directed by
Robert Chetwyn

Incidental music   Set design
Malcolm Sircom   Juanita Waterson

Cast List
In order of appearance

Bill	Robert Gilespie
Alex	Clifton Jones
Rob	John Southwark
Joe	Patrick O'Connell
Mike	Terence Woodfield

The Scene is a bomb site throughout.

> There is only one man in the world
> And his name is All Men;
> There is only one woman in the world
> And her name is All Women;
> There is only one child in the world
> And the child's name is All Children.
>
> *Carl Sandberg.*

Characters:

BILL: A nonentity, aged about forty, fifty. We really find out little about him. Why he is where he is and how he is remains his own secret.

ALEX: A negro, could be any age between thirty and fifty. A giant of a man with immense strength so that everything he does is done with an undertone of violence.

ROB: A priest who felt himself unworthy of his calling and defrocked himself.

JOE: Ex-trade unionist, still ardently believing in the brotherhood of man, socialism and the age of common humanity. Was expelled and imprisoned for appropriating union funds.

MIKE: Aged about eighteen.

SETTING: The scene is a bombed out Church.

Authors Note:-

No matter what the mood of the subject matter during this play, on no account should it be treated with heavy dramatic import until the end.

ACT ONE

At the back there is a crumbling wall, in places low enough for a man to climb over on to the roof of what used to be cellars. Steps lead down to these from this roof which was once the ground floor of the building. When the curtain rises it is late on a summer evening as the play progresses the sky behind the wall grows paler, then darker, then fills an orangey glow as the night city comes to life. BILL is seated in part of the cellars, his back against an arch. He is playing a mouth organ, soft and sweet, the tune nostalgic, something like 'My Old Dutch.' The figure of ALEXANDER appears at the wall, climbs over on to the roof and then down to the cellar. He carries a kitbag over his shoulder. For a moment he pauses, looking at BILL who continues to play, then ALEX swings down his kitbag and seats himself opposite also leaning back against an arch. He watches BILL as he plays and deliberately starts to whistle another tune. BILL after a moment's unsuccessful competition, gives up, taps the spit from the mouth organ with the side of his hand and wipes his hand up his trouser leg. Meanwhile ALEXANDER has stopped whistling and is gazing into the night.

BILL: Why did you do that?

ALEX: Hmn? What you say? I can't hear very well. I gotta sort of ringing in my ear. Don' know, I seem to be hearing mouth organs all day, like it was coming from far away.

BILL: You don't like my playing?

ALEX: Oh, sure, man, sure! You play fine. I just don' like the tune that's all. It's too sad! You wanna play you go right ahead, but play something cheerful, like it's Mardi Gras night an' everything's jumpin' wild.

BILL starts to play an Irish Jig.

Hold it! Hold it, man, hold it! What's that?

BILL: That, my friend, is a bit of Old Ireland.

ALEX: Hmn-Hmn. You Irish?

BILL: Not that I know of.

ALEX: Then what you wanna play an Irish tune for, man?

BILL: The Irish are a tuneful race.

ALEX: Anyhow, that's too cheerful.

BILL: But you said…

ALEX: I said it's too cheerful.

Bill shrugs and starts to play Shenandoah.

Hold it! Hold it! Woah, man! Hold it! Now you gone back to being sad again. Ain't you got no happy medium? I can play better music with my arse. Here give me that thing.

He reaches forward but Bill slips the harmonica into his pocket.

We negroes, we got music, you know? Rhythm, we got it. I mean, like it's in our souls, way down deep. Music for all time. Music to live with, man.

BILL:	Why don't you go and find yourself another cellar then I can play merely to amuse myself?
ALEX:	I like it right here. I feel like company.
BILL:	Well then, having kicked my repertoire for six, what would you suggest as being the most suitable music for this occasion?
ALEX:	Silence, man. Dead, dead silence.

Silence.

BILL:	*(Clearing his throat)* You... think then... that we're dead?
ALEX:	As good as. Guess we can get kicked a bit more.
BILL:	Then as long as we can be kicked we're alive and where there's life there's hope.
ALEX:	Yeah? You can kick a dead mule, don't bring him back to life.
BILL:	But we can come to life again. How do you know we might not be resurrected? Reborn.
ALEX:	I'm tired. You got to be fairly fresh to be reborn.
BILL:	Well, we can still hope.
ALEX:	Yeah. Yeah, that's right. Hope for what?
BILL:	Just hope.
ALEX:	Okay then, we can hope. You bring out your horn and play hopeful music. Start blowing,

	boy, but play music. I don't wanna hear no cats wailing or they get a taste of boot.
BILL:	You name a tune.
ALEX:	Request time. Play a ... Alexander's Ragtime band. Yeah, play that. You know, that's my name, Alexander... play!

Bill plays.

	You got no gaff then?
BILL:	I beg your pardon?
ALEX:	No place to sleep I mean.
BILL:	Why else would I be here?

Starts to play again.

ALEX:	I used to shack up with a white girl you know. She was truly fair, real sweet. I could ha' married that girl.
BILL:	Why didn't you?
ALEX:	She had a brother. He didn't like spades. This was in Liverpool you know. All her family work on the docks there. Well, she's got this brother... real tearaway... about as much guts as a rabbit you know? Anyhow, we all curled up on the sofa one night watching telly and this bantam struts in. 'Hiya, sis!' he say lookin' at me like I was thought up in a horror picture. She gives him a how do you do and me I gave a friendly wave and I say does he want some beer I brought in a couple of bottles. He says no, beer don' agree with him. I don' like this

	wiseacre. He's too smart to be alive. Anyway, we sit there watchin' telly, holdin' hands all nice an' friendly and suddenly this joker, he leans over an' he says 'what's it feel like, havin' the jungle creep all over you?'
BILL:	No! He said that? In front of you?
ALEX:	That was his big mistake.
BILL:	What did you do?
ALEX:	I belted him with the bottle. Have some beer, I said. So that was the sweet frothy end of that romance. Never liked the guy, he was too smart. You know what he used to say? This is on the ball. This is brilliant humour. He used to look all kind a… kind of all a… holy, you know? Then he'd say, 'two things I can't stand, racial prejudice and niggers.' Yeah, okay, you can smile.
BILL:	I'm sorry.
ALEX:	But that used to burn me up inside. Oh, man! I laughed like a good little pet because he was a real joker and he only said it for amusement you know. But that beer bottle sure felt good, yeah!

Silence.

Say, play on, boy. Do I bother you?

BILL: No, you don't bother me. Nobody ever bothers me.

He plays.

ALEX: You done bird then?

BILL: I beg your pardon?

ALEX: No, you never did bird. *(He tosses a pebble)* At least you got four walls in there. You get your Peter an' you know nobody gonna move you for a while. I don' know, man, sometimes I'm thinkin' you're better in than out. Out here you don' know nothin'.

BILL: Who wants to know?

ALEX: *(Tossing another pebble)* I do.

BILL: Why? It won't get you anywhere.

ALEX: I'm getting nowhere fast right now. I'd at least like to see where I'm at.

BILL: I used to think that way. Once upon a time I used to want to know everything. Why it rained yesterday and will it rain tomorrow. Where I come from...

ALEX: Where you come from then?

BILL: ...It always seemed to be raining. They say nature is wonderful in her diversity but sometimes I think she runs out of ideas and then she's like a tired old joke that limps on and on and doesn't seem to know it's a bore.

ALEX: You wanna know something? *(Tossing another pebble)* You talk too much.

BILL: I was given what is fondly termed 'an education.' Most educated people talk too much. It's usually to cover up a lack of

	understanding.
ALEX:	*(Throwing pebble)* I never had no education, not in any school that is, not even in stir, except for needlework classes… ha! ha!

The joke falls flat on Bill who is listening seriously.

	Where I come from, the sun shines all the time, man: shines like crazy. And the water is blue, sooooo blue. And the wind blows cool. The palm trees wave and there's cocoanuts big as your head, and mangoes that smell of turpentine and taste like sweetness itself. And fish! Shark and barracuda like you've never seen, and the sugarcane rolling like a big green sea.
BILL:	Sounds like paradise, if you like that kind of thing.
ALEX:	Paradise, sure. Tin shanties for all. Loquats full of fruit fly and cockroaches so big when you tread on 'em they go crack like you've split a plank. And rats to eat you alive. And the kids all got pot-bellies like they eat too much all the time. And you can catch sandworm and syphilis just by standing around breathing.
BILL:	Well, I've heard it said that variety is the spice of life. And nature has been liberal in your part of the world. You have been lucky.
ALEX:	Lucky? Oh, sure, man, sure! Born in paradise… so first chance I get… I quit. I see the little ships what always come back, so I take a big ship that never go back. That big ship that's gonna take me far away! I was just a kid you know, but I was strong. I thought

she's the most beautiful ship in the world that old tramp. She was so rusted you could hole her with your bare fist, true as God! That old tramp... she roll her way across seven seas like a drunk headin' nowhere. Clanking... man you should have heard that old engine clank!... an' that stack makin' smoke like she was layin' the all time record for smoke screens. *(He stands up looking up at the night)* I'd give my right arm to be back on that ship! I'd give my right arm up to the elbow just to smell her in my nostrils. Just to walk her black decks. Just to sweat out my guts in her rotting stinking choking belly! Man, I'd give my right arm up to here!

BILL: What happened to her then?

ALEX: *(Sitting again)* Down to Davy she go. One day, the old man, he's floatin' high on his favourite dream... big jug of sweet muscatel. He's up above the clouds and we down here with the waves breakin' over her peak like the wrath of God let loose, and down she go that old girl, woosh woosh, clank clank... *(He moves his arm to show a boat pitching in heavy seas, then tips up his hand to show her sliding beneath the waves.)*

Silence.

BILL: She died well.

ALEX: You know? The sea never tasted with salt like the tears we cry for that old lady. But she died well. She wouldn't get two cents for all the trouble to break her up. And the old man went down with his girl an' his jug of wine an' I sure reckon he died a happy man.

BILL: I think if you die happy you stand a better chance of going straight to heaven.

ALEX: How's that?

BILL: I think the angels would welcome a happy face, and what would old Nick want with a smile?

ALEX: If that's the case, then he is wrapped in Abraham's bosom right now, just like in the bible, sweet muscatel, a picture of his lady, an' all. He was a great guy, a really great guy. Nobody would think that if they just saw him but there was nothing phoney about that guy, nothing at all. That ship was his first and last and he loved every inch of her dirty old body and every rivet and every barnacle.

BILL: If you're going to love you've got to love it all, otherwise there isn't much point.

ALEX: Play me a song.

BILL: What do you fancy? Alexander's Ragtime Band again?

ALEX: No. Play me a sad song, a sad sweet song so I can weep and think of that lady, and that skipper who was like a father to us. That was the whole world, man.

Bill starts to play Shenandoah and after a moment Alex sings. As they sit there another figure jumps over the wall and climbs down. He moves towards them hesitantly as he hears the music and then seats himself against the wall Alex is leaning back on so the are actually back to back but not in the same cellar. Alex lifts his hand for silence and the playing stops.

We got ourselves some company. Hey! You in there! *(No answer)* Come out an' lets have a look at you. *(Silence)* If you don' come out we're gonna get suspicious an' you wouldn't like that.

BILL: Maybe it was a rat or something.

ALEX: A pretty big something. *(He leans his head against the wall.)* Friend? *(No answer, he turns back to Bill.)* You know, this is how we used to talk in stir, through solid walls like this. *(He raps)* Is anybody there?

BILL: Leave him alone.

ALEX: If you can answer, move to 'yes!' Hey, you ever play that game, you know, with the letters and the glass upside down? *(Bill shakes his head)* We did it on board ship once only we didn't have no wine glass like you're supposed to so we used a beer mug. How do you expect a beer mug to move except up and down? Anyway we sit there an' nothin' happens see? Then all of a sudden wshhh! Roun' it goes like crazy.

BILL: Yes?

ALEX: Oh, man! Me I'm serious you know but inside I'm laughing! But this other geyser, he's dead straight. 'Is there anybody there?' he say. *(Alex claps his hand and shrieks with mirth.)* Is there anybody there? *(He moves his fingers along a horizontal line as though moving on top of the glass.)* Yes! 'Have you got a message?'... yes! 'What is your message?'

Silence.

BILL: Well?

ALEX: 'Huricane comin'... ship goin' down, all hands!'

BILL: Yes?

ALEX: Oh, man! Me I'm laughin' fit to bust, but inside I quake like jelly. Then I see this greaser, he sittin' there all doubled up so I say 'you been pushin' it!' Hmn! By the time we finish with that greaser he wish he stay away from the spirit world. Say, you got a burn?

BILL: I beg your pardon?

ALEX: Where you been all your life, man? The trouble with you educated monkeys you got no vocabulary! A drag, a cigarette!

BILL: Oh, yes! Of course.

He hands over a packet. Alex takes one and hands the packet back.

ALEX: The funny thing you know, ten minutes later right out of nowhere there comes the biggest blower you ever see an' knocks that old ship all ways at once. Boy, you never see so many scared jacks in all your days.

BILL: Was that the one that went down?

ALEX: No, we didn't go down. We ride through an' when it's all over we find that greaser an' we do him all over again just to show our relief. *(He looks around the wall.)* Peekaboo! I see you!

The man gives a start but otherwise doesn't move.

Say, what's the matter, boy? You in solitary? *(No response. Alex turns back to Bill and shrugs.)*

BILL: Maybe he just doesn't like company. Leave him alone.

ALEX: Why you bein' a hermit in there? Come on out an' be sociable. Join the party.

BILL: Wouldn't it be easier to go around than talk from there?

ALEX: What! An' step out of me own manor? That's not etiquette.

He starts rummaging in his kitbag and produces various tins of foodstuffs.

Little Tommy tucker sang for his supper, what shall we give him?

BILL: Brown bread and butter.

ALEX: Not tonight, music man! Tonight you eat!

BILL: Where'd you get that stuff?

ALEX: Self service store. It said help yourself so that's what I did. But just in case they didn't mean what they said I bought something too. *(He holds up a tube of toothpaste)* Nearly got nicked too. They were mighty suspicious of that little tube of toothpaste lyin' in that wire basket. You got a tooth brush?

Bill shakes his head.

> Too bad! *(He tosses the paste away)*

BILL: *(Moving over)* It's a banquet!

ALEX: Shhh! He might grass.

The man stirs.

> Dig in, help yourself, take your choice. There's peaches, corn, ham, what's this? Frankfurters. Pity we got nothin' to drink but we'll eat good, white man, we'll eat good.

The man rises and stands in front of them.

> Well, look what the smell of food brought out!

Pause.

> Well don't just stand there lookin' at it, man, dig in!

The man sits.

> What do they call you?

ROB: Robbins.

ALEX: Okay, Rob, I'm Alex an' this is…

BILL: Bill.

ALEX: Bill.

ROB: I wouldn't have presumed, but…

ALEX: But you're hungry.

ROB: No, I insist on making a contribution.

ALEX: Another educated gent! Look, what're you standing on principles for? We still got principles to stand on? I don' want nothin' from you. I never ask you to pay for what you eat.

ROB: We pay for everything in life.

ALEX: You goin' preach at us?

ROB: What makes you say that?

ALEX: Because you soun' like it.

ROB: It's difficult to break the habit of long standing.

ALEX: Well stop standing an' sit down.

ROB: I am sitting down.

ALEX: Then eat, and I apologise gents, the silver is a little dirty but the butler is on strike this week.

ROB: I thought I heard you mention you would like a... something to drink.

ALEX: You think you heard right.

With a smile, Rob produces a green bottle from beneath his coat.

Well, take a butchers at that! The boy is a wizard, no mistake.

ROB: It's my contribution.

ALEX: Eat, drink and be merry for tomorrow!...

ROB: Is mothering Sunday.

ALEX: And may our mothers look down on us in forgiveness, for we are their sons, no matter what we done, we are their sons.

ROB: Amen!

ALEX: How come we got all religious at a party, hey? Hey? Come on, let's open the bottle. No corkscrew!

ROB: Oh, yes!

He produces an all purpose knife.

ALEX: Say, you got everything, man!

ROB: No.

ALEX: What ain't you got?

ROB: Salvation.

ALEX: Maybe you get that tomorrow.

BILL: You were a priest?

ALEX: Now then, brother Bill, ain't no cause to ask people their miseries. You just fill your mouth with vitamins an' leave Robbie to do like wise.

ROB: Yes, I was a priest.

ALEX: Well nobody here's goin' hold it against you, boy. You got no cause to fear for that. The past is the past.

ROB: In a way I suppose I still am.

ALEX: What're you doing here then?

BILL: Looking for his salvation.

ALEX: I tell you what, after dinner we'll retire to the music room for cigars an Bill here can give us a little organ recital. The trouble with me is I want all the good things in life an' I got all the bad an' I never could get round to doin' anythin' about it. Say, this is a mighty handy little knife you got here. Got the whole works.

ROB: It belonged to someone. He gave it to me because he wanted me to have it.

ALEX: The most useful thing you ever given I reckon.

ROB: I don't think he had anything else to give. Nothing he treasured as much.

ALEX: Well it's a handy little tool and all.

He stabs a hole in a tin and drinks from it.

Ah! *(Smacks his lips loudly.)* The sunshine fruit! Reminds me of when I was only a kid those days you didn't use to suck from tins. Straight from the fruit, man. You squeeze it, an' you roll it a little, an' you hit it till its all gone soft, then you bite a hole an' suck, an' you squeeze a little, an' you suck.

BILL: You make it sound revolting.

ROB: Psychologists have a name for that kind of thing.

BILL: Psychologists have a name for everything.

ALEX: Don't give me none of that head shrinking talk. That don't mean nothin' to me at all. I do what I wanna do! I don' wanna know why.

BILL: You said you wanted to know everything.

ALEX: *(Shouting)* Not about me! Not about me! I don' wanna know anything!

BILL: All right all right, calm down.

ALEX: Who you tellin' to calm down? You lookin' for trouble? You'll get it, boy. You'll get it good! You... you're abusing my hospitality, that's what you doin'.

BILL: I never said a thing!

ALEX: I invite you to share my grub an' what do you do? Hey? You pick holes in the way I suck oranges!

ROB: Grapefruit.

ALEX: What?

ROB: Grapefruit. It says grapefruit on the tin.

ALEX: I don' care what it say on the tin. You want some? You can have it. I give you some an' I push the tin an' all right down your gullet.

He squeezes the tin into a mangled piece of metal and

drops it at Robbins' feet.

ROB: You're a very excitable person.

BILL: Shall I play some music? They say it has power to soothe the...

He stops dead and looks at Alex who is gazing moodily into space.

Alex?

ALEX: What?

BILL: Did you hear what I said?

ALEX: No.

BILL: Oh, good!

He looks at Robbins who looks at him. Silence.

ROB: If you'll pass me the knife I'll open a tin.

ALEX: You know, this is a real sharp knife.

BILL: You seem to be fascinated by it.

ALEX: Say, where could a man pickup a knife like that?

ROB: I don't know.

ALEX: Where did you say you got it?

ROB: A boy gave it to me. He wanted me to have it.

ALEX: What would you want with a knife like this?

ROB: Nothing. He just wanted me to have it. Something to remember him by. *(Hurriedly)* I didn't do any wrong, I swear it! I never touched him so help me God!

Silence while they look at him.

ALEX: Nobody said you did.

ROB: I know, but it's what people would think, isn't it?

ALEX: Why should anybody think that?

BILL: These days they always think like that, you know what they're like.

ALEX: Yeah, don't we know now?

ROB: They jump to conclusions.

BILL: There ought to be a law against jumping to conclusions.

ALEX: No, we got too many laws anyhow.

ROB: They think because you're a priest you must be blameless. You can't have faults.

ALEX: No! They don't think that.

ROB: Oh, but they do, they do! They forget the flesh is frail. A cassock is no protection, no surety, no bastion against human desires. You have desires like everyone else and they condemn you for them.

ALEX: They think you just got to hide them better, that's all.

BILL: Nobody is perfect.

ROB: Oh, there was one! There was one! He was perfect. He didn't do any wrong and because of that we slew him.

ALEX: Yeah, man, we know all about that.

ROB: That's why we must do right you see, always the right thing. We have to struggle, we have to fight.

ALEX: You been fightin' so hard, man, you gone an' wore yourself right out!

ROB: There was a girl. She was pretty, so gentle. She had eyes like black diamonds and every candle flashed and nestled there and her mouth... her mouth was a rosy mystery that lured a man like a siren's song to dash himself on the rocks of sensuality.

ALEX: Yeah, I read that book once. It was called one thousand and one nights. I loaned it from a guy on a ship once in the Red Sea. You didn't ought to be reading books like that.

ROB: I resisted. The temptation was there but I fought it.

ALEX: Man, if you're down for the count ten to one it's a woman put you there. Now me? I like to see the day a woman put me down if she not gone down first. Tee hee hee! With me they know who's boss.

ROB: You have to be strong!

ALEX: I'm strong. Even when I'm a kid I'm strong. An' I'll show anythin' on two legs in a skirt just how strong I am.

ROB: That's not what I mean. I mean you must be strong to resist temptation.

ALEX: Sure, that's the truth. I resist temptation. I resist like hell! I say to myself, Alex boy, she's goin', any minute now an' she's gone! It's been a tough fight but any minute now, an sure enough, I resist the temptation to quit an' the fruits of the victory are mine, hallelujah!

Silence. Rob and Bill look at each other.

Say, I never tell you 'bout that little girl down in Zanzibar? I remember that one in particular because she so cute, you know? She's only 'bout two bricks high but oh, so round! That girl didn't have one straight line on her whole body, man, an that is a fact. You know what she say to me? Me, I'm struttin' down the street there, all big an' handsome, you know? An' she come scuttlin' up to me all sideways like a crab an' she look up an' she say? You know what she say?

Bill shakes his head.

She look up an' she say – man, this was real cute! – she say, 'You wann take a walk? Rub your belly gainst mine! Soft as silk!'

Rob moves away hurriedly.

An' you know what she say then? *(He follows Rob so that he is practically whispering in his ear, his voice is soft and caressing)* You know what she say then? 'Give you nice French time!'

Alex shrieks with mirth. Rob closes his eyes and sways on his haunches.

	Now where do you suppose she get a crazy idea like that? Hey?
ROB:	How old was she?
ALEX:	Old enough.
ROB:	It's wicked! It's evil that these things should be taken so lightly.
ALEX:	I knows it! Sooner or later this guy goin' start preachin'! Who gave you the right to preach to me?
ROB:	It's lust and fornication!
ALEX:	I know what it is! You think I'm in knee pants or something?
ROB:	Without love it's wrong.
BILL:	So often with love it seems to be wrong. At least it strikes me that way.
ALEX:	Yeah, That's a fact. How a fella know where he stand?
ROB:	She might have been only a child.
ALEX:	Guess that's right. She was pretty small.
ROB:	Like mine… I mean, like the girl I was talking about.

ALEX: She's real? I thought you got her out of a book.

ROB: And the boy. They were both so young and I loved them. Is that strange? To love two wild gentle young creatures at once? Everything is a contradiction. That's why I left, you see. I couldn't bear to see them hurt. I couldn't bear the thought of them growing old, losing their innocence.

BILL: When were we ever innocent?

ALEX: You left because you was scared.

ROB: Yes, there was that. I admit it. I could have done anything with them, anything! I wanted to you see. Yes I did! The world was right to condemn me. I wanted to. My love wasn't pure. We must be pure!

BILL: You can't abide by the opinion of the world, it usually stinks.

ALEX: You can say that again.

ROB: Man is a higher being, a noble creature. We are brothers, all God's children.

ALEX: An' no ole man ever had such a delinquent bunch.

ROB: That's why we must be punished until we do better.

BILL: We been standing in the corner so long now with our faces to the wall, maybe we've grown too stiff to turn around.

ROB: We must do the right thing, or punish ourselves!

BILL: That's dangerous talk.

ALEX: The guy's crazy! You're out of your mind!

ROB: And we must hope.

ALEX: Yeah, there we go again. A little band of hope are we.

BILL: In a wilderness of despair.

ALEX: Keep the white flag flying come what might. Say brother Rob, what you done with your tambourine? You rattle that ole thing a bit an' scare off the boogies. I always been scared of the dark. Things can creep up on you in the dark. Say, you bein' a religious man, what you believe? Did I never tell you 'bout the 'Nerina'? she's a banana boat. I done one trip in her an' I sign off quick. I won't work that ship again if they gave me her cargo as bonus.

BILL: Why? What's the matter with her?

ALEX: She's haunted, man!

ROB: You got proof?

ALEX: With my own two eyes I see that spook. With my own two ears I hear him hollerin' and moanin' with my own two legs I run like hell outa there!

They wait.

One night, I'm due for watch, see? So I'm

walkin' the deck I hears this noise in the hold, see? It's a hot night and the hatch is off so I clambers down to see what's goin' on. I think maybe some of the boys down there havin' a little drink up or something you know? Anyways, I get down among the bananas an' I hear someone moanin' so I thinks maybe someone fall down hold or somethin'. Then I sees it, this fella, lying there all twisted up, all sort of purple in the face you know? He's clutchin' his hand all swollen. I never seen this guy before. Then all of a sudden he sit up an' look straight at me an' he scream blue murder! Boy! I feel like ice down my back an' I'm up that companion like all the devil's in hell on my tail. So I bump into some of the crew. Well, they grab me an' hol' on tight, an' me fightin' an' yellin' like crazy, 'there's a guy in the hold!' I knock a couple of 'em arse over elbow before they get me on deck an' hold me down fast. One guy he sits on my head but we negroes, we got head like concrete, man. Number one, he poke his head over the bridge. 'What's goin' on down there?' he yell. So I tell him there's a guy in the hold an' he ain't a member of the crew an' he look like he's dying. So number one, he come runnin' down lickity spit, an' into the hold he go. Few minutes later he come up. 'No one down there,' he say. They all look at me like I'm crazy or something. 'You been drinkin'?' number one he ask me. 'No, sir! I never touched a drop, so help me!' 'You been dreamin' then,' He say. 'No, sir! I see him! I hear him holler!' 'You take a torch down there with you?' 'No' 'Then how come you can see in the pitch dark?' An' number one wave this torch in front of my moosh. *(Silence)* I saw him. In the pitch dark, I saw him. How do you explain that?

BILL: Phosphorous!

ALEX: In the hold of a banana boat?

ROB: Maybe you were dreaming.

ALEX: I think maybe I'm round the bend or something. All the guys they lookin' at me like I step straight out of a nut house. As true as I'm sittin' here, my face go as white as yours…

BILL: That's some transfiguration!

ALEX: Which is something like a dirty grey considerin' you ain't been washing so good recently.

BILL: I was going today but I lost the three penny bit.

ALEX: He's unhygienic this guy, you know? He don't even have a tooth brush. Say, this seat's getting hard. Must be the springs have gone.

He gets up and crosses to the other arch, resettling himself on a pile of rubble.

Ah, that's better. Now, what was I saying? Oh, yes! About this ghost.

BILL: There must be a rational explanation somewhere.

ALEX: Oh, Sure! Little while latter this old fella, he was chippy's mate but he really too old for anythin' but hittin' the bottle. He tell me the story. Some time back in Trinidad this guy

	he's wanted by the cops, see? So he come on board one night an' hide out in the bananas, figuring' he can eat bananas till he look like one nobody gonna find him there. That okay, ship sail an' nobody find him but... In a banana crate all is not banana, an' one night, digging in to fish himself a nice helpin'... Zit! Old man tarantula get him on the hand. Well, he don't want anybody find him so he lie still an' by the time they hear him yellin' it's too late. An' this is the fella I see lyin' there, holding his hand an' the poison working all over him.
BILL:	I don't believe in ghosts.
ALEX:	You goin' to be one yourself one day so you better start right in believin'... quick.
BILL:	That old chap might have dreamed it all up right out of the bottle.
ALEX:	I didn't dream it.
BILL:	Well... what do you make of it?

Rob shrugs.

	I think you invented it Alex, to try and scare us.
ALEX:	Okay, boy! You can laugh, but when I was little little kid my mother say to me, 'Alex, don't you ever laugh at things just because you don't see 'em for yourself. Things seem strange don't mean they're not true.' In our town there was an Obi man...
ROB:	Superstition!

ALEX: No more superstition than what you been sayin'! This Obi man he could cast spells would make your hair fall out.

BILL: Why should he want to do that?

ROB: If he could cast spells to put hair back he would make a fortune.

ALEX: If this Obi man say you die, you die!

ROB: Superstition!

ALEX: I see it for myself! He say to a fella, die! An' this fella, his eyes go all funny an' he keel right over an' die.

BILL: You believe that?

ALEX: I see it!

BILL: Seeing is believing. But what I want to know is, how much can one really rely on what one sees? People have visions, hallucinations.

Joe enters from D.S. and stands behind Alex.

For instance, I see someone standing behind you. How do I know he's real or only my imagination? In this light it could be a shadow.

ALEX: Someone standin' behind me?

BILL: That's right.

ALEX: Right now?

BILL: This very moment.

ALEX: Right behind me?

BILL: Hmn – hmn.

ALEX: What's he doin'?

BILL: Just standing there.

Slowly Alex turns, sees Joe standing there and with a bound he's at his throat. He hurls Joe against the wall and holds him there with the knife against his chin. Joe is terrified. So is Alex. The other two have been completely taken by surprise at the suddenness of the Negro's move.

ALEX: What you playin' at? Hey? What you mean, creepin' up on us like that?

JOE: I didn't mean anything!

ALEX: You want to get yourself killed?

JOE: I didn't mean anything.

ALEX: That's the right way to do it!

JOE: Help! You're choking me!

ALEX: You play tricks like that you goin' to get hurt bad, you know that?

BILL: Alex!

ALEX: You spyin' on us?

Joe shakes his head, fast getting beyond speech.

BILL: Alex, leave him alone!

ALEX: He's a grass!

Joe shakes his head again.

ROB: You'll kill him.

ALEX: His own damn fault. I can break you in two you know that?

BILL: Alex!

ALEX: I can break you in half. What you mean, scarin' the pants off us like that!

BILL: Alex, I know him. He's all right.

ALEX: *(Letting go)* You know him?

BILL: Yes. He's all right.

ALEX: Peculiar friends you got, creeping around the place.

BILL: I didn't say he was a friend of mine. I just said I know him.

ALEX: Yes? What's his name?

JOE: Joe.

ALEX: *(Swinging back on him and lifting his hand. Joe cringes.)* I didn't ask you.

BILL: His name is Joe.

ALEX: Okay then, Joe, what you doin' sneakin' round like a little slimy toad?

JOE: I was looking for somewhere to kip... sleep.

A pale yellow light suddenly flicks on, flooding the scene. They all turn and look at it.

ROB: *(After a pause)* Streetlight.

ALEX: I know it's the streetlight. You think I'm blind or something?

BILL: He's only stating the obvious. We all do it.

JOE: Well, it's no use staying here then.

ALEX: Nobody invited you.

JOE: Goodnight!

ALEX: *(Grabbing him)* Where you going?

JOE: To look for somewhere to sleep. I'm tired.

ALEX: Now you're here you might as well stay here.

JOE: It's useless. I can't sleep with the light on.

ALEX: I say you stay.

JOE: I suffer from insomnia. I must have the light off or I'll never close my eyes. *(To the others)* All my life it's been like that. I simply can't sleep with the light on.

ALEX: When time comes for sleep I put the light out for you. Sit down.

JOE: Don't you order me about!

ALEX: I said sit down! An' you don't do it quick I knock you down.

Joes sits, immediately, suddenly, on the spot.

>That's better. An' anymore creepin' around you'll wish you'd never seen the light at all.

Silence as the three sit looking at Joe who is embarrassed.

>You another of these here educated gents?

JOE: I beg your pardon?

ALEX: Don't you stand on your dignity with me, boy! You hear every word I say an' you hear good or I'll knock you into the middle of next week.

JOE: Why are you being so belligerent? I never did anything to you.

ALEX: You scared the livin' daylights out of me. I don't like that.

JOE: I didn't mean to.

ALEX: Okay, okay.

JOE: I left school very early but later in life I came to regret it and I believe in self improvement so I took correspondence courses.

ALEX: Didn't have much effect did they?

JOE: Oh, but they did.

BILL: What did you study?

ALEX: Creeping.

JOE: Oh, politics, public speaking, how to gain confidence.

ALEX: You a con man?

JOE: No! Confidence to get somewhere.

ALEX: You got there all right.

JOE: I rose high in the world.

ALEX: An' you fell right down again.

JOE: That was not my fault.

BILL: It never is.

ALEX: You want something to eat?

JOE: No thank you. I see you have some wine there though.

ALEX: No wine.

JOE: Oh, is it finished?

ALEX: No, but it will be, an' not by you.

JOE: I see.

ROB: I think we could let him have some.

ALEX: I said no.

ROB: But why not?

ALEX: Because!

ROB: It's my wine…

ALEX: Your wine? You are mistaken friend, are you

	not? It is not your wine, it is OUR wine, an' I say he don't get any, see? Who say otherwise?
JOE:	Well, I'll be on my way then.
ALEX:	Sit down.
JOE:	I'll never sleep.
ALEX:	It's too early for kip anyway.

Silence.

BILL:	Were you in politics?
JOE:	Oh, no! I only made a study of politics as a background for the work I considered essential. Of course I might have gone into politics later.
BILL:	How did it fit in with your work?
JOE:	*(Looking thirstily at the bottle.)* I'd rather not say.
BILL:	All right. No offence.

Alex, seeing the look, lifts the wine bottle and takes a hearty swig. Joe licks his lips and wipes his mouth with the palm of his hand.

| JOE: | You're not very friendly, are you? |
| ALEX: | After the scare you gave me I'm about as friendly as a king fish. You ever hear about those? Get 'em in South America. Only about this long. *(He indicates about three inches)* You fall in the river with them an' about two seconds flat there your bones all white an' |

clean.

JOE: It's men like you make the world what it is.

ALEX: How's that?

JOE: Yes!

BILL: Don't irritate him, Joe.

JOE: You've got to learn to give and take.

ALEX: With guys like you you preach that but you take all an' you give nothin'. I met a fella once who go round all day talkin' 'bout goodness an' you know how he earn his loot? He sell dirty pictures an' that's a fact. Like our friend here, the dirtier the mind the cleaner the preachin'.

ROB: That's not fair!

ALEX: The louder they holler the more you bet your bottom doller they're hollerin' to cover up. Me? I don't cover up nothin'. You want to know why I'm here? I'll tell you. You want to know?

Silence.

I killed a guy.

Silence.

You want to hear about it?

Silence.

Okay, I'll tell you. It was on my last voyage, see? I been in the nick for G.B.H. an' I'm

	findin' it mighty hard to get a ship. But this Greek skipper…
JOE:	What is G.B.H?
ALEX:	Grievous Bodily Harm. You been in the nick and you don't know what G.B.H is?
JOE:	Who ever said I'd been in prison?
ALEX:	I say so.
JOE:	Well it's a complete and utter falsehood. I could sue you for defamation of character.
ALEX:	You go right ahead and do that small thing.
JOE:	I could too.
ALEX:	Don't tell me! If anybody ever done bird, you have.
JOE:	That is wholly untrue!
ALEX:	There you go yellin' an' tryin' to cover up. You wear the feathers of a jailbird like you were born with them.
JOE:	It wasn't my fault.
ALEX:	An' I bet you got all the privileges. I bet you sucked up every bent screw in the place just for half an ounce of snout.
JOE:	A half ounce is a lot.
ALEX:	Not enough to go sucking up screws for.
JOE:	I don't have to sit here and be insulted.

ALEX: Why'd you come creepin' in the back way? Why didn't you use the front door like everyone else?

BILL: You were telling us about the Greek skipper, Alex.

ALEX: I can't stand creeps.

BILL: The Greek skipper.

ALEX: What?

BILL: Greek skipper.

ALEX: Oh, yes! *(To Joe)* You keep your big mouth shut an' don't ask any more damn fool questions. This skipper he tell me he got a full deck crew but he can do with a galley hand. Well, that better than nothin' so I sign on. The cook is the biggest, dumbest, dirtiest son of a bitch you ever see in your whole life. This bastard he take one look at me an' he say, 'Jesus! I go aroun' seven days a week smellin' dead meat that's turned, now I gotta smell it live!' well, I didn't say nothin' not aloud that is because I don't want to lose that ship but every day this crazy clown he push me. Every day he needle me a little bit more. It's always nigger this an' nigger that.

BILL: Was he an Englishman?

ALEX: I don't know what he was. What difference that make?

BILL: None at all. I was just curious.

ALEX: That guy he push me too hard, that big beefy bastard! 'Hey, nigger!' he say, 'Hey, nigger boy! Get weaving,' he say 'You never done a days work in your whole goddam life. Hey, nigger! Why they let you live, man? You scare the kids with that big buck black pan of yours!' 'You call me nigger one more time an' you're dead, man.' I say to him. 'Okay, nigger!' he say. 'I'm warnin' you!' I tell him. 'Sure nigger, you're warnin' me.' 'Lay off, man, lay off.' 'Okay, nigger!' Nigger, nigger, nigger! That guy needle me, see? I say to myself hold it boy, this white man, he don' mean nothin'. He can't help it, see? But there's only me. There's no one else to say hold it, take it easy. 'What you thinkin' of, nigger?' he says. 'I'm thinkin', man, in one second from now I'm goin' to kill you.' You know what he does? He throw back his head an' laugh, man! He laugh fit to bust. I see them big yellow teeth an' his skin all like turkey flesh. Boy! It's hot down there, one hundred and eight degrees an' me sweatin' like a pig an' suddenly I'm cold, cold as ice, an' there's this meat cleaver in my hand. I aim at his throat, see? Sideways, but he see it comin'. I never see a laugh disappear so fast like it was so scared it run away down his throat. He try to duck, an' like an eggshell, man, like you take the top of an egg... clean as a whistle! He stand there, you know? He just stand there. I want to tell him, pick up your head, man, it's lyin' there on the deck, but he just stand there lookin' at me. so I take him ever so gentle an' I give him a little push over the side, through the hatch he go, an' then I hear the splash. But there's a fella on the next deck havin' a drag an' he starts hollerin' 'Man overboard!' Boy, then I'm scared! So I starts up too, 'Man overboard! Man overboard!'

BILL: Quiet, you'll stir up the whole neighbourhood.

JOE: You'll bring the bogies down on us and they'll get us on a vagrancy charge.

ALEX: *(Whispering)* Man overboard, man overboard.

JOE: I've never kept company with a murderer before.

ROB: What happened then?

ALEX: The while they all lookin' out, I takes the chopper an' the bit of his head an' I toss them out the other side. The old man he stops the ship, swearin' an' cursin'. But they don't find him. Half an hour we sit rockin', the breeze blowin' through, then I hear her starts up. Half an hour, like a thousand years, like no time at all, while I stand there sweatin'. The only way you can tell I'm alive is the sweat. Then I wait an' sure enough, little while I hear them coming. 'What happened?' 'I dunno, man. One minute I'm tossin' out bilge an' the next minute I hears this yellin', man overboard. So I look round an' there's no Sassy... that was his nickname, you know? Sassy... One minute he's standin' by the hatch there havin' a quiet drag an' the next he's gone so I start yellin' too, man overboard! That's all I know, man.'

ROB: They believed you?

ALEX: Ha! They all stand there, lookin' at me, all them white faces, hard like rock. You can see they don' believe me. 'You had it in for him, nigger, didn't you?' Me! I had it in for him! That's a laugh!

BILL: Was he popular?

ALEX: He was white.

JOE: That doesn't preclude the possibility of his being unpopular.

ALEX: Shut up! If you wanna talk, talk sense

JOE: The common man has an innate sense of justice.

ALEX: The common man is common like you an' like you he ain't got no sense at all.

JOE: Men will stand by each other in adversity. The hope of the world rest on that.

ALEX: Christ! Hope again! Ain't I never goin' to hear anything but hope? All a man thinks about is his own dirty hide.

BILL: In a way Alex is right.

JOE: He is not. It's just that we've been led to believe that. It's the capitalists who propagate that theory. Under socialism every man lives for his fellow man. That is his nature.

ROB: Christ said it. Love thy neighbour as thyself.

BILL: Not much use if you don't love yourself.

ALEX: I don't care who say what! I'm tellin' you I'm the only black boy on that ship, an' when the common man come up with somethin' uncommon he don't take to it easy, an' that's for sure.

BILL:	So what happened?

ALEX:	It looked real nasty. They start movin' in. I back up. Any minute now all hell's goin' to be let loose. 'He done him!' someone yell. They all nod like they hope to God it's true. I pick up the coal shovel. Boy, now I'm really wild! I'm crazy mad! 'You come for me, you bastards!' I yell, an' there's goin' to be brains all over the galley!' then the old man, he come down. He ask questions. I know nothin'. Then Sassy's mate he pipes up all clever like. 'Man, how come you're tossin' bilge to win'ard?' Boy, they leap on that like it's the clue to end all clues so I just shrug, figurin' it's best to keep my big mouth shut. Old Sassypants mate, he inspectin' the hull out there. 'No bilge on here,' he say, all proud like. There's a pretty strong breeze but no gash blown on this hull.' 'Maybe I throw it far enough out,' I say. Then someone else chip in. 'How come there's blood on the deck?' 'I been chopping meat, boy, for your dinner.' An' I push the plate right under hid nose. He look at it, an' look at me, an' he turn a little green an' don't say nothin'. The old man says okay he'll make a report, an' that's it. I don't hear another word till we hits port. Man, I hear that hook drop an' I thinks, that's it. An' you know what? There's two cops waitin' there for me. They walk up the plank an' they say, 'You're under arrest.' The old Greek he tell his sparks to wire shore an' they were ready for me. Well, they tried hard, but they couldn't prove a goddamn thing.

BILL:	So you got off.

ALEX:	Got off? Ha! I try for a ship, boy. I hang around

that pool till I'm sick but no ship. Seems no one wants seaman who tosses gash to win'ard.

Silence.

BILL: That's a pretty gruesome story.

JOE: Can I have a drink now?

ALEX: No.

JOE: I won't take much.

ALEX: No!

JOE: Just a sip.

ALEX: Belt up.

JOE: *(To the others).* All I want is a mouthful, just to taste.

ALEX: Quit whinin'.

JOE: I don't understand you, I don't at all. No honestly, I just don't. Unless you're the exception that proves the rule.

ALEX: What rule? What rule? There ain't no rules. You make 'em up as you go along.

BILL: What are you going to do now then, Alex, if you can't get another ship?

ALEX: *(Shrugs)* What're you goin' to do?

Bill shrugs.

How about you?

ROB: I don't know yet. I'm waiting.

ALEX: An' you?

Joe's eyes on the bottle.

I said what are you goin' to do?

JOE: How do you mean?

ALEX: Don't you know it's impolite not to listen when folks talkin' to you?

JOE: I'm thirsty.

ALEX: There's a tea wagon down the street.

JOE: I haven't any money.

ALEX: That's too bad. Well, what're you goin' to do then?

JOE: How do you mean?

ALEX: KEERIST! What gives with this fella? Hey? I mean is he nuts or somethin'? What gives?

BILL: I think you frighten him.

JOE: I'm tired. I want to sleep.

ALEX: You're tired, you want to sleep. You're thirsty you want to drink. You got no cash. You got no ideas. You got rules nobody understands. You sittin' here on your hands like four penny hambone with a crowd of bums...

BILL: Steady on!

ALEX: ...talkin' crap! I ask you a simple question an' you can't answer it!

Pause.

JOE: Would you mind repeating the question please?

ALEX: Sure, I'll do that. What are you goin' to do now?

JOE: I'd like to go to sleep.

BILL: *(Hurriedly)* He means, having got yourself into the position just described, what are you going to do about it?

JOE: Oh, I see! Well why didn't he say that in the first place?

Alex looks around extending his arms in a gesture of complete bewilderment.

ROB: Well what are you going to do?

JOE: I shall re-establish myself of course.

BILL: Of course.

JOE: With the aid of my fellow man I shall once again take my place in society.

ROB: But society has rejected you.

JOE: Only temporarily. You can't believe they would reject me forever!

BILL: You've come to an amicable arrangement I

	suppose.
JOE:	Well, that's what I went to prison for, isn't it? Isn't it?
BILL:	I don't know. I've never been to prison.
JOE:	But that's the whole idea, isn't it?
ALEX:	There you go again. Look, the guys that send you to stir, they're strong, man! When they make the rules you don' argue, you just lose right down the line.
JOE:	All I need is a chance to prove myself.
ALEX:	With a record?
JOE:	Until I made a mistake I had a clean and unimpeachable character. I made a mistake that's all.
ALEX:	Yeah! You got nicked!
JOE:	I've paid for it. I've had my punishment. My debt to society is settled.
ALEX:	Don't you believe it, man! Don' you believe that for one second. Once they put the finger on you, they'll hound you down, an' hound an' hound…
JOE:	No!
ALEX:	Because it makes them feel good! It makes them feel big! It makes them feel tall to know they better than you. They don' forgive an' they don' forget.

BILL: If our prisons weren't full our lunatic asylums would be.

ALEX: There's got to be a fall guy! There's got to be a stooley! Somebody somehow got to take the rap.

JOE: No, you're wrong. They'll help me.

Alex snorts.

Oh, but they will!

ALEX: Okay then! Go on! There's the world. It's waiting for you with lovin' arms outstretched wide! There it is! Take a look! Go on out an' see what happen!

Joe doesn't move.

JOE: You can't expect me to do anything constructive in the middle of the night.

ALEX: You think the world sleeps? Never sleeps, boy. Always got one eye on you, waitin' for you to take one step out of line and... Zit! *(Clicks his fingers)* Got yer! How long you been out now? *(Pause)* How long?

JOE: About six weeks... approximately six weeks, yes.

ALEX: Ha! What is this approximately, huh? What's this mean? You know to the minute how long you been out. The day you come out is a red letter day. It's right here! *(Touches his forehead)* Oh, sure, you don't remember the day you are born, or the day you are baptised, or the day you lay your first woman, or your

	wife's birthday, or your weddin' day, but this day you remember... how long?
JOE:	Seven weeks, three days, twelve hours... approximately.
ALEX:	Okay, good enough. You tried for job yet? *(Silence)* Look man. How come you don' answer questions? You tried for?...
JOE:	I heard you! I heard you the first time!
ALEX:	That's right. So you did. *(To the others)* An' he still wants to believe they gonna help him. Ha! You been a bad bad boy an' you're in the doghouse, an' that is where you gonna stay!
JOE:	No!
BILL:	Give a dog a bad name.
JOE:	That's just the point, I'm not a dog.
ALEX:	To the other dog you are a dog.
JOE:	I'm a human being with rights!
ALEX:	Oh, Sure! Your book of rules it say you got rights, but the big big pity of it is... the other fella' he don' read no book of rules.
JOE:	And I've applied to the union for resumption of membership. After all I did them good service. I was a good member. I paid my dues. I stuck to the rules. I stood in the majority. I rose in the ranks. I was highly efficient and responsible shop steward.
ALEX:	An then what happen? *(Silence)* Go on, Say!

	(Silence) You don' want to say?
JOE:	I'd rather not thank you.
ROB:	Was it drink?
JOE:	What makes you think that?
ALEX:	The way you look at this. *(He taps the bottle)*
JOE:	No, it wasn't drink.
ALEX:	Okay, let it ride. He don' want to say he don' want to say. Sure we not interested.
BILL:	I am.
ALEX:	Well nobody interested in what you're interested.
BILL:	In that case I think I'll take a little stroll. I feel the need to stretch my legs.
JOE:	So will I?
ALEX:	Hey, where you fellas all goin'? What you runnin' away from?
BILL:	We aren't running away. We just want to take a walk, that's all.
ALEX:	Okay, I come walkin' too.
JOE:	With us?
ALEX:	Sure with you! Why not? You think I'm ashamed of you or somethin'?
JOE:	Well, no…

ALEX:	Maybe you ashamed of me, huh? Maybe you don' want to be seen, steppin' out with a nigger.
BILL:	No, that's not so at all. But what about all your things? If you leave them here they may get lifted?
ALEX:	They were lifted in the first place so what difference. I tell you what, we finish of this bottle of wine first then we walk, huh? How's that? Here... *(To Joe)*... there's a little in the bottom still. Come on, man, sit down an' finish the wine. An' look at all this grub we left. You ain't eating a thing.

After looking at each other for a moment they all sit down.

JOE:	You don't like being on you own, do you?
ALEX:	When I'm on my pat I feel like... like I don' know nothin'... like I wanna cry out, you know? Maybe I been in the stir too long. Drink up, boy, drink up.

Joe takes a swig.

	I feel like someone he's looking over my shoulder all the time, like someone watchin' me.
BILL:	Did you ever have that dream when you were a child, that something is chasing you and you don't know what it is. It's right behind you, you can feel it there. You try and run and your legs won't function. You try to scream and you open your mouth and can't make a sound and all the time you daren't look around to see

	what it is.
ALEX:	No, I never dreamed like that, but that's how I feel sometimes.
BILL:	Then just as it gets you, you wake up. Did you ever dream that?

Rob shakes his head.

	I dreamed it a lot as a child. Just recently I find I'm dreaming it again. Maybe it's a kind of premonition. Maybe it's going to catch up with me, and this time... this time I won't wake up.
ALEX:	You see? You see? You tell me I'm supposititious. We all got it.
JOE:	I haven't.
ALEX:	You! Here give me that. *(He snatches the bottle)* You drunk the lot, you bastard!
JOE:	You offered it to me.

Alex hurls the bottle away.

	Now why did you do that?
ALEX:	Because my rule book it say I should belt you one.
ROB:	It's all right there was no deposit on it.
BILL:	There might be one on his head though.
JOE:	You know it is extremely fortunate that the future welfare of society doesn't depend on

	people like you.
BILL:	Very fortunate… for us.
JOE:	If everyone believed as you do and carried on like that we'd be in a sorry state wouldn't we?
BILL:	But we're in a sorry state as it is.
JOE:	Yes, but it's sorting itself out, isn't it?
ALEX:	Okay, you wake me up when it's all sorted out.
JOE:	I believe there are many people, in the common run, who have the right ideals, who are willing to help, who are willing to stoop and lift up the man who has fallen.
BILL:	The price is too high.
JOE:	I believe in the brotherhood of man. Liberty, equality, fraternity.
ALEX:	They send you to stir an' you believe all that?
JOE:	Why not? I'm not embittered by prison, why should I be? I'm not ashamed. I don't believe the stigma will remain. I believe in the dignity of mankind.
ALEX:	Ho! Ho! Ho!
JOE:	You can laugh.
ALEX:	I am laughing.
JOE:	I believe…

ALEX: You believe in fairy tales.

ROB: You believe in Obi men.

ALEX: Obi man is fact, fairy tales isn't.

BILL: Remember mother's advice.

ALEX: Okay Okay! What is this dignity then?

BILL: Dignity is what a man stands on when he has nothing else left.

ALEX: Yeah, like our friend Joseph here. He stands so much on his dignity he got the worst case of flat feet you ever seen.

JOE: There's nothing wrong with my feet.

BILL: He's speaking metaphorically.

JOE: Oh!

ALEX: You know? Some places I been I seen little kids, little tiny kids, starvin', beggin' in the gutters. That is most dignified.

BILL: Where was that?

ALEX: I dunno. Some place I been.

ROB: I hate to think of children suffering.

BILL: I think the most dignified set of people I've ever seen was once when I plucked up enough courage to enter a Turkish bath. All those fat pink sweaty bodies oozing about the place or being walloped by a beefy masseur. That is a truly edifying spectacle.

ROB: Opposite my church there was a public house. I used to watch the drunks at closing time, how they stood around as if waiting to be sculptured.

ALEX: Or sick.

ROB: As though they were posing. Or when they moved, the way they carefully picked each step, gently gently, in slow motion almost, very graceful.

ALEX: When you seen a couple a hundred guys locked up with their own smells an' their own miseries, week after week, then you seen somethin'.

BILL: Would you call a whore dignified?

Pause.

ALEX: Ever seen a rough up on the street? With the carvers? That is really something.

BILL: Fear.

Pause.

ROB: Lust?

Pause.

ALEX: Ever seen a mob gone crazy? Man, I'm tellin' you. I seen it. A whole screamin' yellin' wild mob. It happen when we were in Durban once, 48? 49? I don' know, how it all started. One fella he tell me little black boy he get kicked in the arse by this Indian fella. That's all, man. Nex' thing you know the whole town gone wild. The black man he swarmin' all over knockin' hell outa any Indian he see. Then the white kids come out with their bicycle chains just to join in the fun, then the cops knockin' hell outa anybody, then the army and then the navy, all trigger happy guys. Man, what a night, shootin', burnin', lynchin'. Everybody busy beatin' up everybody else an' nobody knows why. They get one of the guys off the ship so a couple of his mates, we go look for him. So many get knocked off that night the goons got no place to lay 'em all out so we go along lookin' for this buddy you see an' there are all these stiffs laid out nice an' tidy. I see a couple of kids there got caught in a burnin' bus. Man, they not only look like roast chicken, they smell like roast chicken. Boy! I puke out my guts everywhere. Ain't never had a taste for roast chicken since that day.

BILL: Did you find your buddy?

ALEX: Oh, sure! They done him up good and proper. A stiff is a dignified thing.

JOE: You're all discussing the wrong things. You're not being fair. You're talking about abnormal circumstances. You're talking about the abnormal.

BILL: We're talking about people.

ROB: We're people.

ALEX: We got dignity. Boy, you ever been to Birkenhead? That's a great town you know. Straight straight streets, miles long, real planning. The houses are so small even the mice got hunch backs. I'll tell you what though, they got hot an' cold runnin' women in each room.

Rob is not amused.

          Why that's a real dignified town, man!

BILL: Just think, millions of years of history and evolution have been recorded just to bring us... *(He looks around)* ... four people together in this place at this moment.

ALEX: What for?

BILL: That, you will have to ask history. But it is a thought for sombre and proud reflection, to fulfil one's destiny.

ALEX: We should have a flag!

BILL: A dignified one, not to imperialistic.

ALEX: Claim our independence.

BILL: And send dignified diplomatic notes.

ROB: Then the communists would try to step in and ruin everything.

ALEX: Let 'em try! They muscle in on my republic I show 'em who's boss. Say, we could do that right here, right on this spot!

BILL: No, sooner or later they're going to clear this up and turn it into a parking lot, and you can't fight progress.

JOE: You are all talking rubbish.

ALEX: Is that so?

JOE: Childish rubbish! Why don't you grow up? Why don't you mature?

ALEX: You're so mature you're shrivelled up.

ROB: The Italians say, if a man hasn't a little of the fool in him, he's only half a man.

BILL: That's right. Make believe, pretend. You can't be dignified and tell yourself the truth the whole truth and nothing but the truth so help you God, least of all yourself. Well, think I'll take that little walk.

ALEX: Hey! Hey! How about some music? This guy plays the mouth organ real great you know?

Bill looks embarrassed.

ROB: Is that so?

BILL: Well...

ALEX: Sure! That is a fact. Come on, boy, let's have some music.

JOE: Can you play 'Bless this house?'

BILL: That's not exactly appropriate, is it?

JOE: It's my favourite.

ROB: I'm very fond of plain chant.

BILL: I'm sorry I can't oblige.

ROB: *(Hopefully)* I like Palestrina too.

Bill smiles and shakes his head in apology.

ALEX: Say, what you do with yourself all the day?

ROB: Me?

Alex nods.

I spend a lot of time in churches. Every time I pass one I step inside and meditate a while. I like going to the cathedral, especially when the choir is practising. I sit and listen. All that wonderful sound, the organ and the boys' voices, soaring upwards. It seems so pure.

ALEX: I stand 'round the pool mos' of the time. Chew the rag some. Play a little game of cards maybe.

JOE: Time hangs pretty heavily.

ALEX: Yeah, that's right. That's the only true thing you said yet. You get pretty chokka.

JOE: When I see all those queues at the labour exchange, I feel... it makes me feel rather desperate.

ALEX: Say, aren't we a real bright bunch then, hey? Me lookin' for my ship that ain't comin', old Robbie here lookin' for his salvation. You lookin' for the milk of human kindness when the old cow's milk is all curdled up. How about that? What you lookin' for, Billy boy?

BILL: Hmn? Nothing as far as I know.

ALEX: You're a lucky guy, not that I believe you.

BILL: It's the truth, I think.

ALEX: What you do all day then?

BILL: I'm an expert on building sites.

ALEX: Come again?

BILL: Yes indeed, I know every building site in town. Some of them aren't worth more than three minutes, others are good for continuous performances and repeats. They really cater for the viewing public. Glass enclosed observation platforms so the dust doesn't get in your eyes, flowers in boxes, plans and drawings of what's going on. Oh they do it in style. Draw good audiences to. I do feel however that though the visual aspect is so good one is missing something from the auditory angle. I feel that apart from the natural sound effects like automatic drills and various four lettered Anglo-Saxon words, there should be a kind of commentary by the overseer or foreman or someone. You know... a... 'Down below to your left you will see on the concrete mixer, Bill Jones, aged forty three married with six kids has been with the company for an accident free twenty five years and except for a tendency to use his mixer as a waste disposal unit is something of an expert in his field. Now up above you to the right you will see George Smith. George is a bricklayer of, if I may use the word without offending our brothers in other unions...

JOE: Do you mind!

BILL: '... class! Note the nonchalant way he flicks off unwanted cement, and note with what supreme ease he breaks a brick in half with his trusty trowel, a gift I may say of the company in recognition of his service in ending the strikes of 1923 by leaving the bricklayers union and joining the concrete workers union where he rightfully belongs. The fact that he is still laying bricks is incidental. With him you will see his apprentice, seventeen year old Charlie Brown. Charlie is wearing the regulation blue denims and boots in which I may say he looks very smart and a true son of the proletariat. I may add that it took some persuasion by the management to get him out of his skin tight shot satin and winkle pickers, but when he was warned he might slip off the scaffolding and break his pimply neck he readily agreed to the change. A very stubborn young man is Charlie Brown. He is unfortunately a replacement for Edward Montgomery Smythe who yesterday dropped a brick on the Architect's head. Edward insists it was an accident. His hair, he says fell into his eyes. However he has been temporarily suspended while the unions discuss his case. He was actually fired but the men tried to use his dismissal as an excuse to strike for an extra ten minute break and in order to avoid this, the management have suspended him on full salary. Interviewers will find him at Fred's caff in the high road where he is not doubt indulging his pals in cokes and glorifying British Labour by continuous insertion of sixpenny pieces into the Jukebox thus ensuring the rising prosperity of the café owner, who is incidentally, Maltese and has an interesting sideline in curious... ha ha!... affairs. Ahem!'

JOE: You are despicable.

BILL: Well it would make it interesting, wouldn't it?

JOE: Scab! Blackleg!

ALEX: Don' you talk to my friend like that!

JOE: Just because you don't believe in the solidarity of the working classes.

BILL: I'm a willing dupe of the fascist hyenas!

JOE: You don't seem to realise how the masses have been exploited! You know nothing of the class struggle.

BILL: All right you lower middle class intellectual…

JOE: Working class!

BILL: …what do you know? Apart from what you've heard at your red lectures.

JOE: I am not a red!

BILL: Agitator!

JOE: I believe…

ALEX: Oh, belt up!

JOE: I will not belt up!

ALEX: You belt up or I'll send you to Coventry!

ROB: Gently, gently.

JOE:	What am I doing here anyway?
ALEX:	I'll sing you a little song.
JOE:	I don't want to hear any song.
BILL:	Sing the Red Flag.
JOE:	I want to help you, I really do. I want to show you the facts.
BILL:	You don't know the facts. You stopped living thirty years ago.
JOE:	And all you do is gang up on me.
ALEX:	I'll sing you a little song I made up.
ROB:	If it's obscene I don't want to hear it.
ALEX:	A fine bunch of comrades you lot are.
BILL:	Sing us your song if it makes you happy.
ALEX:	*(Singing)*

> Yesterday her hair was yellow as corn,
>   Today it's ruby red.
> The day before it was strawberry roan,
>   But as we lay in bed,
> I could see, oh brother,
>   Oh, brother I could see,
> The roots were black jet black,
>   Oh brother the roots were black jet black.

JOE:	I knew it! I just knew it!
ALEX:	Yesterday my love was as sweet as the rose,

>   A rose without it's thorn,
>   But now I drift any way the wind blows,
>   With sails all tossed and torn,
>   For I found, oh brother,
>   Oh brother yes I found,
>   Her heart is black jet black,
>   Oh brother her heart is black jet black.

Bill has started to accompany him on his mouth organ.

>   Yesterday I fell for that colourful dame,
>   Who's name is lady luck.
>   And now my gambling is never the same,
>   I lose my every buck,
>   For she's led oh brother,
>   Oh brother how's she led,
>   My soul to hell and back,
>   Oh brother my soul to hell and back.
>
>   So although her hair is as shiny as silk,
>   Her eyes a china blue,
>   Her skin as soft and as tempting as milk,
>   Don't let her capture you,
>   Stay away, oh brother,
>   Oh brother stay away,
>   Her heart is black jet black,
>   Oh brother her heart is black jet black.

In the distance there is the sound of a police whistle. They listen.

>   I hear the bogey man.

The sound is repeated. This time nearer. They listen again.

BILL: Yes, well I think I'll take that little walk then.

The sound is repeated nearer.

JOE: It is always unpleasant and embarrassing to be picked up on suspicion for somebody else's misdeeds.

ALEX: Agh, you don' wanna be scared of them. What can they do? We ain't done nothin'.

BILL: You'll have to explain your shoplifting expedition.

The sound is repeated, very close.

ALEX: Ha! Nobody got proof I didn't pay for that stuff.

There is a sound of running and the whistle is repeated. One by one the men rise and leave in their own manner. As soon as the stage is empty, Mike enters over the roof and scrambles down. He is sobbing with exhaustion and throws himself into the cellar where he cowers in a corner. The whistle and feet running pass by and disappear into the night. Panting he waits until there is silence, then he drops forward and buries his head in his arms.

ACT TWO

A little later. Mike is seated on a pile of rubble scraping out the remains of a tin with Rob's knife. He tosses the tin away and starts on another just as Bill enters above and comes down the stairs. Hearing him, Mike silently puts the tin down and gets well back in the corner. Bill comes into his line of vision, and looking straight ahead pauses to fumble for his cigarettes.

MIKE: Stay there!

BILL: *(After leaping a few inches from the ground)* Who's that?

MIKE: Don't move.

BILL: I'm standing dead still after having been nearly killed with fright anyway.

MIKE: I thought you were a cop.

BILL: Do I look like a cop?

MIKE: I didn't see you, I heard you. Anyway, how do I know you aren't C.I.D?

BILL: Do I look like C.I.D?

MIKE: You can't tell for sure.

BILL: Then why don't you search me to see if I'm carrying a badge?

MIKE: Funny ha ha! Big joke!... who are you anyway?

BILL:	My name is Bill if that makes any difference. What's yours?

Silence.

	Can I move now?
MIKE:	I suppose so. But don't try anything funny. No tricks I mean.
BILL:	I assure you I don't know any tricks, least of all funny ones. I see you've made yourself at home.
MIKE:	This your grub?
BILL:	No, not exactly.
MIKE:	I was hungry.

Bill nods and seats himself.

BILL:	You're very young.
MIKE:	So?
BILL:	Where did you get that rig out from? You look like a refugee from a jumble sale. Was that you the police were chasing a short while ago?
MIKE:	You ask too many questions.
BILL:	I beg your pardon. I didn't mean to pry. If you're still hungry, carry on eating. Don't let me disturb you.

Mike takes the tin and continues to eat. Bill watches him.

You are hungry.

MIKE: That's what I said.

Alex leaps over the wall and comes clattering down the steps. Mike drops the tin and leaps to his feet.

MIKE: There's someone coming!

BILL: Oh, it's only Alex.

MIKE: He your mate?

BILL: Hardly. An acquaintance I would say.

ALEX: *(Seeing Mike)* Who's this?

BILL: The latest addition to the family. I don't know what he's called yet.

ALEX: Yeah? What's your name, kid?

MIKE: Who you calling a kid?

ALEX: You. What's your name?

MIKE: What's that to you?

ALEX: Nothin'. You the guy the cops were after?

MIKE: What if I am?

ALEX: Nothin'. *(Pause)* Why you lookin' at me like that?

MIKE: That's my problem.

ALEX: Oh, a fly guy, huh? You watch it, boy! You put out too much lip you get it chopped off.

MIKE: Is that so?

ALEX: That is so.

BILL: Steady Alex. We don't want another murder tonight.

ALEX: I ain't done one yet, but maybe I'll get around to it if the mood so takes me you know?

MIKE: Big deal!

ALEX: Look sonny, why don't you go home to mammy?

MIKE: No home, no mammy.

ALEX: Well go find yourself one then. We don't like strangers.

MIKE: I got nowhere to go.

ALEX: That… is your problem.

MIKE: You want me to go?

BILL: It's immaterial to me.

MIKE: Is he really a murderer?

BILL: That he is indeed.

MIKE: You're kidding.

BILL: Am I?

MIKE: You're having me on, aren't you?

ALEX: You want me to prove it?

MIKE: *(Brandishing the knife)* You stay away from me!

ALEX: Hey! What you doin' with Robbie's dagger?

MIKE: Stay away! Don't you come near me.

ALEX: What's the matter, tough boy? You scared a little?

MIKE: You come any closer I'll slit you from ear to ear.

ALEX: *(Laughing)* You frighten me!

Joe enters.

JOE: I'm back!

ALEX: Jesus! I thought we'd lost you. Say, how come you keep using the tradesman's entrance? Why don't you use the front door like a civilised human being?

JOE: I forgot.

ALEX: You forgot, you forgot.

JOE: Anyway, I felt I would like to come back and continue our discussion.

BILL: That's what you think.

JOE: Who's this?

ALEX: It's the kid from next door. He came over to play.

Joe nods.

	What you done with Robbie then?
JOE:	I left him down the road talking to some children.
ALEX:	Kids shouldn't be out this time of night, it's unhealthy. That goes for you to.
MIKE:	Thank you very much.
ALEX:	Where's your old lady?
MIKE:	How would I know? Mooching around with some drunken slob I suppose.
BILL:	You shouldn't say things like that.
ALEX:	That's disrespectful.
MIKE:	It's true anyway.
ALEX:	Where's your old man then?
MIKE:	Which one?
ALEX:	The one that mis-begot you.
MIKE:	Tell me what he looks like and I'll tell you if I've seen him.
ALEX:	You mean you're a bastard?
MIKE:	No! No I'm not. I'm legit and I've got a birth certificate to prove it.
ALEX:	That's nice.

MIKE: And my old lady was all right, let me tell you. She was okay was my mum until it got too much for her.

BILL: Until what got too much?

MIKE: All she had to put up with after that husband of hers walked out on us when I wasn't even born yet. He didn't even know what I was going to be. He didn't even know I was on the way and he walked right out! Fancy just walking out on your wife like that, no reason...

BILL: There's always a reason.

MIKE: It's all his fault. What a lousy character he must have been. Boy, if I ever catch up with him, oh, just wait! You just wait. I'll catch up with him and... and... you wait.

ALEX: What'd he look like?

MIKE: I dunno. Something like me maybe. S'funny thing you know? My old lady, she didn't keep any pictures after he scarpered. Not even a wedding picture.

BILL: So you don't even know what he looks like?

Mike shakes his head.

ALEX: Some job catching him then, hey? You better start lookin' right now, here, take some provisions for the journey.

MIKE: You really want me to go?

ALEX: Look, kid, the cops are on your tail. They still

	be snoopin' round an' I for one am lookin' forward to a night of undisturbed shuteye.
JOE:	You won't forget to put the light out will you? Otherwise I won't get a wink all night.
MIKE:	Let me stay, just a little while, please! I won't stay long. If we hear the cops I'll scarper quick.
ALEX:	You'd better. Well? What you all say?

Bill shrugs.

	Brother Joseph, cast your vote.
JOE:	I er… I vote he stays. After all, he seems to be one of us.
ALEX:	Okay!
MIKE:	Thanks!
JOE:	What's your name, son?
MIKE:	Mike.

Joe nods.

ALEX:	This old man of yours…
MIKE:	Nah, let's not talk about him. He's just a dirty word.
ALEX:	Maybe he found another woman.
MIKE:	No.
BILL:	You shouldn't get so upset about it, Mike, after all, there must have been a reason, people don't

just do these things. *(No response from Mike)* I knew a chap once, he was married quite young and everything on the honeymoon was fine, but when they settled in their new house he found one of the wedding presents was a cuckoo clock. Well cuckoo clocks are fine if you happen to like them and he had no particular aversion to them, except this one. It had a cuckoo that popped in and out quite normally every hour but underneath it had a little boy on a swing instead of those sort of pendulum things, and little boy in a green hat and white stockings with a sort of silly smile on his face, I remember the smile particularly it was such an idiotic grin. Anyway, this little boy used to go up and down, up and down, up and down, tick tock, tick tock, up and down, until it nearly drove him mad, so he said to his wife, the cuckoo clock has to go. But it can't she said, it's from Aunt Minnie. I don't care if it's from the Archbishop of Canterbury, he said, it has to go. Well, she was adamant, it stayed where it was, so one night coming home in the dark he tried to knock it off the wall, but all he succeeded in doing was falling over a chair and breaking three ribs. So he said to his wife, either that clock goes or I go, I give you three days. At the end of three days he packed his bags and went. So you see, there is always a reason.

MIKE: You call that a reason! That's the daftest tale I've ever heard yet. He must have been barmy to walk out just for a thing like that.

BILL: No, no, I think he had every reason to act as he did.

MIKE: Then you're as bloody cuckoo as he was. If my

	old man walked out for a reason as silly as that and I found him I'd do him good and proper, I would an all.
ALEX:	What happened to the wife?
BILL:	*(Shrugging)* Still dusting the cuckoo clock I suppose. I wonder if she threw out the wedding pictures too.
MIKE:	If she had any sense she would. No point in remembering a crazy clown like that. Blimey! I've heard of some but that one takes the biscuit! Listen!
ALEX:	What's the matter?
MIKE:	I thought I heard something.
ALEX:	Say what're those goons chasin' you for anyway? You done up an old lady or something?
MIKE:	Nah! I'm not like that. Nah, what'd I want to do a thing like that for?
ALEX:	Loot.
MIKE:	Easier ways of getting loot than beating up old ladies. Some old ladies are pretty tough. If they're anything like my granny… there was a right one for you… if that old girl gave you a wallop across your lughole you had a bee in your bonnet for a week. Anybody try anything on her, ninety she was, and she'd belt 'em black and blue. Say, are you really a murderer?
ALEX:	What's it to you? You thinkin' of shoppin' me

	or something?
MIKE:	Course not! What do you take me for, copper's nark?
BILL:	This discussion in criminology is slightly above me, shall we get back to my plane?
MIKE:	All I want to know is whether he really done it. Maybe he just dreamed it all up.
ALEX:	Anybody else tell me tonight that I dream things and I'm goin' to go crazy!
JOE:	He does confess to killing a man though I cannot see that that is cause for boasting. From my point of view all killing is fratricide. You see, I believe…
MIKE:	You really did it?
ALEX:	You sound keen, man. You want to try?
BILL:	God forbid!
JOE:	Yes indeed. We see enough trouble as it is.
ALEX:	Nobody knows the trouble I've seen, nobody knows but Jesus.
MIKE:	How did it happen?
JOE:	Thank you very much, we've already heard the whole sordid story once this evening, we don't want to hear it again.
MIKE:	I do.
ALEX:	No no, brother Joseph for once is on the ball, I

	ain't in the mood right now.
JOE:	*(Seeing Mike's disappointment)* If you must find someone to hero worship why don't you find somebody worthwhile.
ALEX:	You kiddin'?
MIKE:	Yeah, such as who?
JOE:	Karl Marx.
ALEX:	Crap!
JOE:	There you go again!
BILL:	Happy as can be, all good friends and jo…
JOE:	Taking the mick…
MIKE:	Watch your language! You're talking about the man I love.
JOE:	…out of things you don't understand just because you have no social consciousness.
BILL:	Politics bore me.
JOE:	That is because you have no social consciousness.
MIKE:	What's that when it's at home?
JOE:	Selfish, that's what you are!
BILL:	There are only two kinds of politicians, those with too much sincerity and those with none at all! The one is as bad as the other.

JOE:	I give up.
BILL:	Good! And about time too.
JOE:	No! I don't mean that I give up.
BILL:	Then say what you mean.
JOE:	I mean that you're beyond it.
BILL:	That's right, so give up.
ALEX:	He don't look beyond it to me. I wouldn't give up trying.
JOE:	Oh, your mind just runs along one track.
MIKE:	Tell me about this guy you done in.
JOE:	And so does yours.
MIKE:	Who asked for your opinion?
JOE:	I did you a favour young man, you might remember that.

Mike makes a rude gesture.

	Well that's gratitude for you!
ALEX:	No more'n you can expect.
MIKE:	Alex?
ALEX:	Yeah?
MIKE:	Tell me about it.
ALEX:	There's nothing to tell. He weren't worth the

	air he breathed, man.
JOE:	And that is a misconception for a start, if he…
ALEX:	Look! The only misconception around here is you! So why don't you hole up your ugly gob before I do it for you? Because every time you open it you make me puke! BELT UP!
Silence.	
JOE:	Why do you get so violent?
ALEX:	When you kill a pig all you lose is the squeak and that goes for you too so don't you push your luck, boy, that's all.
MIKE:	I nearly done in a screw this afternoon.
Pause.	
	I did!
JOE:	One would think he owns this place the way he carries on.
ALEX:	Billy boy, why don't you play us some music?
JOE:	Carrying on like a maniac, threatening everyone.
BILL:	I don't feel up to it.
JOE:	Abusing his privileges as a member of the community.
MIKE:	It was like this you see, they were taking us down to the country in an open van you know?

ALEX: No, I don't know.

JOE: He should be ostracised, sent to Coventry.

Alex picks up a stone and hurls it at Joe. It misses Joe's head by inches. He yells. Mike laughs.

ALEX: You goin' to shut up now?

Joe pulls himself up and looks at Alex.

MIKE: I mean like the van's got bars an' all, but it's got windows, instead of like the Maria that's all blacked up, and they were carting us off in this wagon, see? *(Pause)* Well all I can say is when they cart kids around in open charas for everybody to gawp at they ought to be ashamed of their selves, didn't they. That's a horrible thing to do, isn't it? I mean there you are, an' everybody can look in an' see them carting you off.

BILL: Five minutes later they wouldn't know you if they passed you in the street.

MIKE: Yeah but even so that's a terrible thing to do. It's like the old days, isn't it? Like the French revolution and the trumbils an' all, with the old women sittin' there knitting. Or like they used to have a public hangings and everybody coming out to watch, and then they carve you up and hang you all over the fair like it's a bleeding butcher's shop!

JOE: Do you mind!

MIKE: And you sit there and you see all the people walking about outside and there's your freedom out there. You see it passing you. And you stop at the lights and sit there while the screws crack jokes and you make out you don't care and you're bored and it doesn't matter a tinker's curse what they do to you. But outside you can see the mobs and they can look in and see you and that is a terrible thing.

ALEX: You take this ride today?

Mike nods.

ALEX: What'd they nick you for?

MIKE: I lifted sixpence off a newspaper stand.

ALEX: What did you get?

MIKE: Six months.

ALEX: It was a damn fool thing to do anyway.

MIKE: Yeah, I know, but honestly I didn't have a penny, I was skint. I'd been on probation you see, for forgery, I forged signatures on a couple of cheques at this place where I was working. Oh, I suppose I deserve what I get, I've been bad I admit. Before I was living off deserters. I had this basement place and there was about five deserters used to kip there every night. I didn't ask them how they got their money, I just lived off it. Sometimes I'd go out on a booze up with them and I'd get some old geyser talking while they lifted his wallet. Yah, I suppose I deserve what I get only when it comes… *(He shrugs)* Anyway, after I got caught about the cheques. I went to work in this shop, one day I met one of these guys. He asked me to loan him a fiver. I told him I haven't got it so he says I'd better get it or else. So I forged this cheque. It was dead simple so I did another, then another until one day the boss says he'd like a little word with me so I go into his office and there's these C.I.D an' that was it. Well, I got another job but in a few days there's this telephone call, anonymous, and the boss gives me my cards on the spot.

ALEX: Well, Brother Joe? What do you say to that, man?

MIKE: It was the same every job I got. This joker phones up the boss when he finds out where I am and he says, ' I suppose you know the kid working for you has a criminal record.' So I have a jaw with my probation officer and he say it's best to tell 'em first I got a record, so what happens? This git saves himself a lot of fourpences.
Well you can't live off the dole and there I was, no place to go, nothing to eat and skint, so I lifted this tanner. Next thing I know two guys come up to me right out of nowhere. 'We're police officers.' All very lahdy dah and posh, you'd a thought they sweated eau de cologne the way they looked down their noses at me. 'How much money you got on you?' 'Sixpence ha' penny,' I tell 'em. 'Lets see it.' Sure enough, back of the sixpence there's this little blue mark. 'You'd better come with us,' they say, and bob's your flippin' uncle! The beak, he looks at me and he says, 'Young man, you have quite a record. We have tried putting you on probation and it doesn't seem to work. I have no alternative but to use sterner measures. If I could order a whipping I would.' You'd think I'd murdered his flippin' grandmother or done his daughter in the bath

or something the way he carried on, proper aerated he was an' all! 'You must realise,' he says, 'that society is not going to tolerate your kind of behaviour and I have no other course open to me but to send you to prison. I hope never to see you before this bench again.' So do I you old bastard, I thought. You want me to be like you? Sitting up there all high and bloody mighty...

JOE: He's only doing his job.

MIKE: Who's side are you on anyway, their's or ours.

JOE: I was only pointing out...

MIKE: And like those bleeding screws behind me, just waiting to haul me out to the chara and off to choky! You want me to be like that? I'll go inside for ten years I won't be like that shower!

JOE: Big talk but it's all talk.

MIKE: You think so?

JOE: I do.

MIKE: Then what's that?

He moves over to Joe and holds out his arm.

JOE: It's a scar.

MIKE: All right then, don't say I'm all blab. I don't ask for it easy, mate. I've never asked for that. I seen too much trouble to hope for it easy. All I ask is to have it straight, that's all. And I haven't seen that yet.

ALEX: Okay, brother Joe?

JOE: He's young. He'll learn. You've got to belong, and to belong you have to abide by the rules, that's all.

BILL: Didn't the probation officer say anything on your behalf?

MIKE: Oh, yes, 'I would like to point out to the court,' he says, 'that this boy has had no home life to speak of and he has never known what it is like to have a father who might install a little discipline.' To which his lordship replies, 'Then maybe prison will make up the er… deficiency.' Yeah, that was the word he used, deficiency. He was right I guess.

BILL: The magistrate?

MIKE: No, the probation officer. He was right. Maybe if I'd had an old man, maybe I wouldn't be where I am today. Still, what's the difference, they get you in the end, either way.

BILL: But it seems as though they haven't, not at the moment anyway.

MIKE: Well, we stopped at the lights, see? And one of the kids suddenly he starts bawling his head off, just yelling and yelling. I don't know, maybe he suddenly got more sorry for himself than we were for ourselves, maybe just seeing all that freedom passing by. I know this kid kept on saying he was framed. 'I'm innocent!' he said. Funny kid, you know, little redhead half-pint with no front teeth… nice kid. 'Why would I do a thing like that?' he kept

	on saying. 'I wouldn't do a thing like that! Is that worth losing my freedom for? All I want,' he says, 'is the blue skies above me, that's all I want, just the trees and the wind and the blue skies above me. I wouldn't throw away that doing something stupid.'
ALEX:	What did he do?
MIKE:	Oh, they got him on a receiving charge. Some pal of his, leastwise I don't think even he was a pal, just some guy who needed a gaff, this guy bedded down in his shack one night with about fifty tickers and half a dozen radio sets and left them under the bed. But the cops got on his trail so he did a bunk pretty nifty like, then when this little redheaded guy gets back there the cops are waiting for him. 'I didn't do it,' he says. 'I'm not interested in money, what do I want with money? All I want is the trees and the grass and the blue skies above me.' If he said it once he said it a hundred times. Then he starts up this howling. Well, the screw doesn't go for this so he leans forward and starts to rough him up a little. Then one of the other kids, dark, quiet number you don't ever notice, suddenly, wham! He bunny punches this screw and down the old nit goes. I don't think this guy really wanted to do it you know? I think he was more surprised than anybody. Anyway the other screw starts wading in so the guys in front come leaping around to offer assistance and the next thing I know I'm haring down the road like a bat out of hell, and there's yelling and this kid still sitting in the corner saying, 'All I want is the trees and the blue skies!' I kept on thinking about that. Boy, my hearts going like a Sherman tank and my legs feel like they been

through a wringer but I keep on hearing this kid howling… and here I am.

BILL: With the blue skies and the trees.

ALEX: Yeah! You sure picked the right spot for a picnic, man.

BILL: How long do you think your freedom is going to last?

MIKE: What's the odds? Maybe tomorrow, maybe the next day, who cares?

JOE: It hasn't done you any good, running away.

MIKE: I know that. I'm not daft. I didn't stop to think. But I still got friends, I can hang out for a while.

JOE: Can you rely on them?

ALEX: You're a right one to ask that.

MIKE: Yeah, one or two, I think. There's this dame. *(He laughs)* Oh, you should meet this girl, she's a one and no mistake. Her old man's doing five years for housebreaking. The day he got sent up she says to me, 'Mike,' she says, 'Let's you and I go cheer ourselves up, life's too short.' So we go along to this club and this bird, Lorraine her name is, she get's as slewed as a newt. 'Hey, Lorraine!' I say, 'Lorrie, come on, let's go home.' I could see any minute something's going to happen with her in the pickle she was, and sure enough, suddenly she stands up and she yells, 'My life is ruined,' she yells, 'Finished! They've taken everything from me, even my poodle!' and she dropped

	the lot! Blimey! There she stands, starkers as the day she's born, bawling her flippin' head off. Well I got her wrapped up with the willing help of half the club and into a cab and put her to bed. 'You're a good boy, Mike,' she says, 'You're a good pal, I won't forget you.'
BILL:	After that little spectacle I'm sure she won't.
JOE:	Your trouble seems to me, is that you've been mixing with entirely the wrong sort of company.
ALEX:	No worse than you.
JOE:	On the contrary, and I don't like to go on having to contradict you, but the people I knew were hardworking, industrious, trying to better themselves... why are you looking like that?
ALEX:	I just don't know how anyone can be so stupid. It's way way beyond me, man. Haven't you learnt anything at all?
JOE:	Of course I have.
ALEX:	Well it certainly don' sound like it. You talk the biggest load of bullshit I ever hear.
MIKE:	She was a bit of all right that girl, let me tell you. When I was on holiday camp she was the only one ever wrote me a letter. I still got that letter. 'Hope they're treating you nicely, Mike.' She says. Nicely! Huh! 'We're going to make an honest man out of you, son.' Says the big white chief, 'We're going to teach you an honest trade.' 'Oh, yes.' I say, 'And what are you going to teach me then?' 'Carpentry'

	he says. 'That's nice,' I tell him, 'And what are you going to teach me when I run out of fingers?' honest trade!
BILL:	I would say you know, that you have natural criminal tendencies.
JOE:	No such thing as a natural criminal. Anti social behaviour is a product of environment.
ALEX:	You know something, if this empty vessel carries on making so much sound, I'm going to fill it in good an' proper an' that's a fact!
BILL:	I thought you said you were on probation.
MIKE:	Yeah, I was. For forgery.
BILL:	Then what were you in borstal for? At least that I take it was what you were referring to as a holiday camp.
MIKE:	Oh, that was for breaking and entering.
BILL:	You've led quite a full life, haven't you?
MIKE:	Suppose I have at that. Never had a motor bike though.
BILL:	What's that got to do with it?
MIKE:	Always wanted a motor bike. A five hundred job. Just imagine that! Pull on the clutch, slip her into gear, open the throttle, grrrrr! Always see myself on a motor bike. Maybe go in for racing one day.
BILL:	It's the modern short cut to a juke-box Valhalla so why not?

JOE:	The way you're carrying on you're not likely to get a motorbike for the next ten years at least, not the way I see it anyway.
MIKE:	Well what do you suggest I do then?
JOE:	Give yourself up for a start.
MIKE:	They want me, they can come and get me, see? Ain't that right then?
ALEX:	Why not?
MIKE:	I'll tell you why not?
ALEX:	Nobody wants to know.
JOE:	I've had enough of you.
ALEX:	And I've had a bellyful of you too.
JOE:	Well this time, I am going to say what I intend to say and you try and stop me.

Alex moves. Joe picks up a handy size rock. Alex stops.

	I don't like you. You do nothing but cause trouble.
ALEX:	*(Holding out his hand)* Give me a butt, Bill.
BILL:	Got no more left, sorry.

Alex moves back into his original position.

JOE:	If you try anything on me you big bully I'll let fly with this rock. Bill will back me up, won't you, Bill?

BILL: Me? I haven't said a word.

JOE: You've got to back me up. He's a menace.

BILL: Yes, maybe so, but a... I'm not exactly what is called a fighting man.

JOE: Neither am I, but I've had enough of his browbeating. So I'm going to tell you, Mike, why you should give yourself up. And I'm going to tell you, you big bully, so listen.

ALEX: Okay, I'm listening.

JOE: He's in trouble, right? Right. But not so deep he can't get out, not yet. And the deeper he gets the harder it's going to be for him, and getting out is the most important thing. Isn't that right, Bill?

BILL: It all depends.

JOE: A rock can fly in two directions and I'm getting tired of you too. Who do you think you are?

BILL: I'm nobody.

JOE: Sitting on the fence trying not to live. You can't live on a fence, you're not a rooster. If you're alive you've got to live with people, it's living with people that matters. So come down and tell me, am I right?

ALEX: Well, Billy boy? Is he right?

BILL: Look, what does it matter what I say?

MIKE: It doesn't matter at all because it isn't going to make the slightest bit of difference. I told you, here I am and here I stay and when they come I'll run like hell and if they want me they got to run faster than me, that's all.

JOE: They will. And you'll go on running and running and always they'll run faster than you. They'll catch you up every time. As our friend here would say, you're on the losing side.

MIKE: Well, who put me on the losing side to start with, hey? Answer me that. That old man of mine, that's who! He started running first the old bastard! He got me up the creek. If it hadn't been for him I wouldn't be here at all. Why don't they catch up with him then, hey? Why don't they?

BILL: Forget the past, Mike. You're still young enough to have a future.

ALEX: What brought you off the fence?

BILL: Not like us. We're too old.

ALEX: Speak for yourself.

BILL: Too tired. You can still do it. You can still have that motorbike, or any of the other things you dream of. For us they're just dreams, for you they can still come true.

Pause.

MIKE: No. You got it all wrong, mate. No, not for me. I don't believe it. I know what I am. I'm fixed. I'm like that kid in the truck. The first chance

	he gets to have blue skies and trees over his head, he won't be able to see them for six feet of solid earth. What's the use?
BILL:	Just to be alive, that's the use. Not like us who've thrown it away. Like the savage who finds a pearl and never realises its value.
MIKE:	Yeah, yeah, I know! I appreciate what you're trying to say, I do honest, that's a fact. But look what if no one gives you a pearl in the first place.
BILL:	Why wait to be given it? Go out and find it. If you can't find it, make it.
ALEX:	Mike, you an' me, we're in the wrong company, boy. What do you say we team up, huh? You an' me. I know a nice little tickle down by the docks. It's dead simple…
JOE:	NO!
ALEX:	Who you yellin' at?
JOE:	No… please! Mike… Mike listen, I read something once…
ALEX:	I bet you did!
JOE:	Mike!
ALEX:	An' if it's like the rest of the stuff you been spoutin' you know what you should have done with it.
JOE:	I forget where I read it or who said it…
ALEX:	*(Standing)* You coming?

Mike starts to rise. Joe grabs his arm

JOE: There is only one man in the world, and his name is all men...

ALEX: Lay off the kid. He doesn't want to hear all that crap.

JOE: There is only one woman in the world and her name is all women...

ALEX: That's a fact!

JOE: There is only one child in the world, and the child's name is all children. Mike, you are that child... you are Mike! Go back. Take what they hand out. It doesn't matter how you feel about it now, take it. And when it's all over, try, Mike... just try it!

Mike is genuinely moved by this and looks doubtfully from one to the other. Even Alex is sullen and silent for a while, then Mike removes Joe's hand, still on his arm.

ALEX: Why don't you leave the kid alone? You're getting him all confused. You're blowing a whole heap of hot air! Now cut it out! He don' wanna hear it.

BILL: How do you know what he wants to hear?

JOE: A long while ago, Mike, I was working in a factory...

MIKE: More mug you!

JOE: I earned my money every week...

MIKE: I bet you did!

JOE: Good money too with overtime.

AlEX: What do you call good money, man? I like money that shouts out loud. You earn that kind in a factory? Huh! The kind of money you get there talks in little little whisper. That don' mean nothin'.

JOE: I was an official of my union, treated with friendliness and respect.

BILL: And dignity.

JOE: All right, you think it's very funny, but I don't. Those things mean something to me, they mean a lot to me.

ALEX: If they mean so much how come you're here?

JOE: Because I did a very stupid thing.

ALEX: And knowing you, that weren't too difficult, hey?

JOE: I took some money. I got into debt and to get out of it I took some money. Money that had been entrusted to me by my fellow workers.

BILL: Why do you always have to sound like a left wing pamphlet?

ALEX: How'd you get in the red then?

JOE: That doesn't matter anymore. The fact is it was a lot of money and I took it. I hoped to put it back before I was found out but I couldn't. so that's why I am here.

ALEX: That is a sad story. My heart bleeds for you. See that? See how my heart bleeds?

JOE: The fact that I went to prison is no punishment compared to the shame I feel in letting down my comrades.

ALEX: Only because they'll never let you forget it.

JOE: The men I worked with day by day, shoulder to shoulder.

ALEX: Look, if you tell us a story tell it, you don't have to get up on your soapbox.

JOE: Men I laughed and joked with... It was their money, their trust, and I betrayed it. You can't do something like that and hope to get away with it. You got to pull with the rest. You've got to help them, and they've got to help you. It's the only way.

ALEX: All the worlds a little queer, save thee and me, and even thee's a little queer. You know who used to say that? Little guy I know on the China run. He had two things were the pride and joy of his life, a book by some old Roman fella and a beat up old cat he used to call by the same name as this Roman fella. This beat up old cat got no ears and no tail. Got 'em tore off in a fight I suppose, man, that was a real wise pussy! Every time we hit port that old cat sits by the gangplank and soon as it's down, off he goes to find himself a lady cat. I bet that old bastard got more kittens than any cat I know. Every time we hit port the old boy, he'd look at his cat and he'd say, 'remember old Roman fella, all the worlds queer save thee and me, and even thee's a little queer.' He never make any friends. Only got his book an' his cat. Time come for the ship to sail, sure enough up the plank walks this cat all smiles like he just done up every lady cat in town, an' the old boy walk away knowin' his Roman fella back on board an' all is okay. If you can find a guy like that beat up old piece of fur then I can believe what you say, but you won't ever find a guy like that.

During the above, Robbie has entered and now appears before them.

        Well, well, it's old Roman fella. You just missed the big confession.

ROB: I don't take confession anymore.

ALEX: Oh, well, you'll probably get a repeat anyway. Where you been?

ROB: Talking to some children down the road. The children in this neighbourhood certainly know some terrible language.

BILL: Products of their environment.

MIKE: Children anywhere know some terrible language. At least all the children I've met.

ROB: Who's this?

ALEX: His name's Mike. He's on the run.

ROB: From the police?

MIKE: Well what do you think I'm on the run from? Kindergarten? Oh, we've got a right one here!

	Who is he, anyway?
ALEX:	He's a priest.
MIKE:	Oh! You doing charity work then?

Rob shakes his head.

	What you doin' down here then? I thought you one of these coves goes around you know, dishing out coffee and buns with prayers.
JOE:	He's on the breadline, like us.
MIKE:	Oh, what, have you been given the push then have you? They fired you then?
ROB:	Not exactly.
MIKE:	You been caught doin' naughty things? Lots of that these days aint there? Don't know what the worlds comin' to, I really don't.
ROB:	You mustn't think the worst of people.
MIKE:	Oh, I don't. I just take them as they come. *(Silence)* I suppose you know all the wrinkles?
ROB:	Wrinkles?
MIKE:	Bout God an' that. You being a priest I mean.
ROB:	Well if I do, I certainly haven't been able to iron them all out.
MIKE:	Never held with any of that religious stuff. I mean it's okay for them that do. Takes all kinds to make the world I always say. Even flatties got to eat I suppose. But it don't make

	sense to me, I mean all that psalm singing an' wailing an' that. What do you say me old china?
ALEX:	Don't ask me, I'm superstitious.
MIKE:	Yeah. Well my old lady's like that, dead superstitious an' all. Sleeps with a China man every time she can. Brings seven years good luck she says.
BILL:	Has it?
MIKE:	Not that you'd notice. But then it's to make up for all the bad luck she gets every time she breaks a mirror.
BILL:	How often does she do that?
MIKE:	Every time she sees a China man. *(He laughs)* Oh, excuse me, padre, I forgot.
ROB:	That's all right. I see you have my knife.
MIKE:	Hey? Oh! Oh, yes... here.
ROB:	No, I don't want it. You keep it.
ALEX:	You giving it to him?
ROB:	Yes, he can have it. I don't want it anymore.
ALEX:	How do you like that! Doesn't even know the guy and he gives him his knife!
BILL:	Love at first sight.
ALEX:	And a heathen into the bargain! How come you didn't give it to me? Your buddy! Your

	tried and trusted old friend!
BILL:	You're an even bigger heathen.
ROB:	I don't know. It was just an impulse. Sometimes people need to be given things. Is there any food left?
MIKE:	Yeah, there's a tin of something here, shall I open it for you?
ROB:	Thank you.
ALEX:	Hey, steady there, what you donin' boy? You thinkin' of teamin' up with him? Oh, man! You don't wanna do that. You take my warnin', boy, he's the most dangerous of them all. These two got nothin' on this specimen. This one will get you for sure.
MIKE:	Look, all I'm doing is opening him a tin of grub, that's all. What's wrong with that?
ALEX:	It's the first step in the wrong direction, that's what's wrong with it.
MIKE:	Why?
ALEX:	He's buying you.
MIKE:	Ah! All he did was give me his knife. That was a pretty decent thing to do.
JOE:	And what about me giving permission for you to stay with us?

Mike repeats the gesture.

Well!

ALEX: Well what can you expect with all the guff you been spouting? You wanna hear the way this guy's been shootin' off his big mouth!

Mike passes over the tin.

ROB: Thank you.

ALEX: Hey, Mike! Let's you an me go and chase up a couple of birds.

MIKE: Don't be daft. If I put my nose out of here I'll get nicked.

JOE: You're going to get nicked anyway.

BILL: You're only delaying the inevitable, like going to the dentist.

MIKE: Well let me have my last wild hilarious fling without hearing a lot of preaching. I dunno... Seems to me like everyone always wants to tell you what to do an' nobody knows anyway.

ALEX: What about Lorraine?

MIKE: When I go there I go on my pat. Anyway, what you on about?

ROB: You don't seem to like my friends.

MIKE: Oh, there okay! A bit screwy, but okay.

BILL: Thank you very much.

ROB: What have they been telling you?

MIKE: They been saying I should go back. Give

	myself up.
ROB:	It's the only sensible thing to do.
MIKE:	You think so?

Robbie nods.

	Yeah, I suppose you're right at that. *(Pause)* It was very nice of you to give me this.
ROB:	They won't let you keep it though.
MIKE:	You bet they won't. It can go in with my personal belongings. There isn't much to go in anyway.
ALEX:	Yeah, an' before that happens they'll have you on another charge, being in possession of a dangerous weapon.
MIKE:	Okay, I'll leave it somewhere. Then when I come out I can pick it up.
ALEX:	Leave it with me. I'll keep it for you.
MIKE:	Knock it off! What do you take me for?
ALEX:	I wouldn't like to say.
MIKE:	Proper narkey, en' he?
ALEX:	I offered to team up with you, didn't I? Hey? I offered to take you on a little job.
MIKE:	*(Ignoring him)* You shouldn't have given it to me though. I don't deserve it.
ROB:	The best kind of presents are the one's we

	least expect.
MIKE:	Yeah, but you mustn't think I'm better than I am.
ROB:	I never thought that.
MIKE:	I wasn't misled you know. I knew what I was about. Believe me I deserve everything I get. I know I done wrong.
ALEX:	This is getting like a bloody Sunday school treat. What's the matter with you guys? You make me feel sick. What you got to feel so grateful for?
MIKE:	Well! It's a peach of a knife an' all. Look, it's got the lot.
ALEX:	So it's got the lot! Well shut up about it then! You carryin' on like an old woman with guts ache.
MIKE:	*(To Rob)* Thanks. *(Silence. Mike looks around him, then stands up.)* Well I suppose I'd best be going.
ALEX:	Where you going?
MIKE:	Find the nearest copper, the smaller the better, and hand myself into his tender care. See you when I get out.
ROB:	I hope so.

He walks away from them stops, stands a moment and comes back. Sitting down again.

ALEX:	Enjoy your trip? *(Silence)* Didn't get very far,

	did you?
MIKE:	It's against human nature that's what it is. *(Pause)* It is! Just going and handing yourself over to a cop like that. Blimey! It's like cutting off your arm! You try it.
JOE:	I don't have to.
MIKE:	Okay then, you have a go! See what it's like.
ALEX:	I ain't runnin' away.
MIKE:	No. I can't do it. I just can't do it. How can you expect me to? It's unnatural. What do I say to him? He'll think I'm proper balmy won't he? Please, Mr Policeman, I been a bad boy, you got to take me in.
ROB:	Just tell him who you are and what you've done.
MIKE:	Please, Mr Policeman, my names Mike, I done in a screw and beat it out of a maria but I've seen the error of my ways and here I am to take my punishment like a man so kindly escort me to the nearest cop shop and lock me up until such times as I stand in that bloody court and that old beak looks down his long snoot at me and tells me I'm the scum of the earth and it's high time I ran out with the ruddy bath water.
ROB:	I'm sorry, Mike.
MIKE:	You're sorry! Thanks mate, thanks for nothing. So am I, I'm sorry too believe me. I'm more sorry than what you know. I wonder what's happened to that little redheaded half pint.

You think he's still yellin' 'bout the trees and the blue skies? No! I can't do it!

ALEX: Carry on makin' so much row and the bogies will get you right here.

MIKE: I'll nip over to Lorrie's, she'll put me up a couple of days.

JOE: If they find you there you'll get her into trouble.

MIKE: That's a fact. I'll stay here a while then.

BILL: You'll get us in trouble.

MIKE: Proper old nuisance, aren't I? There's got to be someone who wants me!

ALEX: That's right, man. The cops.

MIKE: Someone else I mean.

JOE: Someone will, when you're in the clear.

ALEX: Haven't noticed anyone wantin' you in particular.

MIKE: Belt up! I don't want to hear any more! I can't do it an' that's all there is.

ROB: Would you like me to come with you?

MIKE: Where to?

ROB: The police station, I'll come with you.

MIKE: What for?

ROB:		Well, I thought it might be easier if I went in and explained while you waited outside.
MIKE:		No! If I've got to take it I take it on my own. I don't need anyone to do the explaining for me.
ALEX:		If you left it to him you'd probably get another five years.
ROB:		It was only a suggestion.
MIKE:		I got to think. There must be a way. Maybe I can get out of the country or something. They don't have to catch up with me. I got this far.
JOE:		You don't stand a chance.
MIKE:		There must be a way.
BILL:		There's only one way.
MIKE:		You! Why don't you shut up and leave me alone? I got to think. I got to find a way.
ALEX:		You come down the docks with me. I'll show you the way.
MIKE:		What if I get pinched?
ALEX:		We won't. It's dead easy, man. Then you can lay up for a couple a days. I flog the stuff, you get your share, then you can beat it. What you say, boy? Dead simple.

Mike turns away.

You scared?

MIKE: Yeah. I'm scared all right. I'm scared of the bluebottles, and the beak. I'm scared of the court, and the screws and the prison. I'm scared of being locked up every day, day after day. I'm scared all right. *(To Rob)* What do I do?

ROB: I told you. It's the only way.

Mike looks from one to another.

MIKE: What do I do?

ALEX: If you're so yellow you shouldn't have paddled your canoe up the creek in the first place. I'm tired. Reckon I'll get a bit of kip.

ROB: I have an idea, what if you went somewhere, as though you were hiding, then I could tell the police where you are.

MIKE: Shop me?

ROB: Tell them, that is with your permission, if you wanted me to.

MIKE: I don't see the point.

ROB: That way you don't have to give yourself up and you don't lose face, if that's what you're worried about.

MIKE: No, there's no sense in that! Is there? I mean I might as well wait until they get me anyhow. I don't want them to find me! What do you think I did a bunk in the first place for?

ALEX: Because you were scared.

MIKE: ALL RIGHT! *(To Rob)* All right.

ROB: Where will you be?

MIKE: Down the corner, by the café. Up that little alleyway there.

Rob puts his hand on Mike's shoulder. Mike doesn't move.

ROB: You'll be all right, Mike.

Mike still doesn't move. Rob gets up and goes out.

ALEX: You gone crazy? You goin' to let him do it?

MIKE: Why not?

ALEX: Why not! Jesus, I should break every bone in your body, you little crumb! You goin' to give in without a fight?

MIKE: Nothin' to fight.

ALEX: You got loose, didn't you? You can stay loose.

JOE: Leave him alone.

ALEX: You come down to the docks with me...

JOE: Leave him alone.

MIKE: That old man of mine, the bastard! If that old man of mine had been around to give me just one thing, like he done, stead of running out on us like he did. Wait till I catch up with the old nit... you wait. I wouldn't be in this mess if it weren't for him and that's a fact.

JOE: Seems to me most people shouldn't be allowed

	to have children, the way they treat them.
BILL:	You can jail a man for lacerating his child's body with a buckled belt. Can you jail him for lacerating his child's mind? Too often it's done in ignorance.
JOE:	Oh, you've come off your fence again have you?
MIKE:	Every time I mention my old man he comes off the fence. You'd think he wanted to protect him.
BILL:	Forget him, Mike.
MIKE:	How can I? He got me in it.
BILL:	You can't know that for sure. It won't do you any good, making yourself remember it all the time.
ALEX:	You're a great one to talk, you are.
JOE:	Yes indeed. Listen to all the things he's been saying. You can tell he's just not one of us by the things he's been saying.
MIKE:	Yeah, you and your bleeding cuckoo clock! You ever hear the likes of it in all your life!
ALEX:	How come you run away from a little thing like that, man?
BILL:	Who said it was me?
ALEX:	You did.
BILL:	I did!

ALEX: You did.

BILL: I never said anything of the kind. I said a chap I knew…

ALEX: I remember what you said. I'm the kind always remembers.

BILL: What did I say?

ALEX: 'I remember the smile,' is what you said.

BILL: The smile… such an idiotic grin.

MIKE: You ran out, just like my old man.

BILL: Yes, I suppose so.

MIKE: Why?

BILL: I told you why.

MIKE: There was no reason.

BILL: Hadn't you better be getting down the alley? Rob's probably found a policeman by now.

MIKE: You want to get rid of me, don't you? You didn't want me to stay in the first place. Why?

ALEX: He's scared of you. Maybe he's your old dad.

MIKE: Nah!

ALEX: Could be, he's about the right age I reckon.

MIKE: Nah! He couldn't be my old man, he's too soft.

ALEX:	Your old man ran out on you. He left you in the cart, didn't he? Like this one here.
JOE:	Yes. No sense of responsibility you see. No social consciousness.
ALEX:	How do you know you ain't Mike's daddy, hey?
BILL:	Don't be absurd!
ALEX:	Don't forget he never knew 'bout his kid, don't forget that?
MIKE:	Yeah, didn't even know what I was going to be.
JOE:	Parents like that should be found and severely punished by law for all the misery and harm they cause. Look at this poor kid here...
BILL:	I'm going for a walk.
ALEX:	You runnin' away again?
BILL:	I'm going for a walk.

As he moves, Alex puts out a foot and down Bill goes. The three of them laugh.

ALEX:	Enjoy your trip?
BILL:	Mike, I'm sorry that you are in so much trouble.
MIKE:	Everyone's sorry for me, all except my old man.
ALEX:	No, no! This is your old man saying he's sorry.

MIKE: Well being sorry is not enough.

BILL: But there's nothing I can do for you. I know how you feel…

MIKE: You know nothin'!

ALEX: You're just an old bum sitting on your jack spoutin' a load of bull an' I for one am tired of you.

BILL: Good night!

ALEX: Hey, wait a minute! Where you goin', man? You just walkin' out on us? Just like that? Like you walk out on your wife an' your kid?

BILL: To my knowledge I never had a child.

ALEX: Now wait a bit, wait a bit. We want you to stay around? Don't we boys?

MIKE: Yeah.

All three have risen and are standing around him.

JOE: We want you to show us how easy it is to run away.

BILL: I'm free to come and go as I please.

JOE: Oh, listen to that! He's free! Yes indeed. Free to run away from responsibilities. Free to sit on the fence and ignore people like us.

BILL: Excuse me.

ALEX: You ain't goin' no place, man. Mike here

wants to have a little word with you, don't you Mike? Here, talk to your daddy!

With a powerful shove, Alex hurls Bill towards Mike. Mike, seeing him coming holds out his hands as though to ward him off. In one hand is the knife. The whole thing is over in a flash. Bill sinks to his knees, clinging to Mike, then drops. The three men stand stock still.

JOE: What happened? What's happened?

MIKE: I didn't mean it. I didn't mean it. I forgot about the knife! I forgot it was there. I didn't mean to hurt him.

JOE: Is he dead?

MIKE: I didn't mean it, honest to God! What would I do a thing like that for? I didn't want to kill him! It was an accident. I didn't know you were going to do that! You pushed him.

He turns to look behind him where Joe has been standing.

You saw…

But Joe has gone.

You saw him push… push him.

He turns back. Alex has gone; Mike is alone with the knife in his hand and the body at his feet. He looks around him desperately, and then sinks to his knees besides the body. From off stage, Alex's voice can be heard singing.

ALEX: Yesterday I fell for that colourful dame,
    Who's name is lady luck,
And now my gambling's never the same,
    I lose my every buck.

> For she's led oh brother,
>   Oh brother how's she led,
> My soul to hell and back,
>   Oh brother my soul to hell and back.

As the sound of his singing dies away, it is topped by a mouth organ playing a melody soft and sweet and nostalgic as the curtain comes down.

Other Titles Available

Plays

Are you Sitting Comfortably
Au Pair
Beautiful For Ever
Between Two Sighs
Early One Morning
Generations
Hear the Hyena Laugh
How do you Like your Wagner
Little Footsteps on the Petals
Oh Brother!
Red in the Morning
Rosemary
The 88
Third Drawer from the Top
Thriller of the Year
Twilight of Aunt Edna
Women Around

Musicals

Black Maria
Champagne Charlie
Cupid
Fugue In Two Flats
La Belle Otero
Peter Pan

For information on this
or any other available plays please contact:

info@dcgmediagroup.com   www.dcgmediagroup.com

www.ingramcontent.com/pod-product-compliance
Lightning Source LLC
Chambersburg PA
CBHW020011050426
42450CB00005B/412